Infrastructuring

THEATRUM MUNDI

Contents

4	Introduction
10	Doing It Yourself/Together/With Others (DIY/T/WO)
	A conversation with Sean Roy Parker
22	Breaking Cultural Infrastructure
	A conversation with Cecilia Wee
34	Museum Cultures
	A conversation with Meneesha Kellay
46	A New Cultural Institution
	A conversation with Marta Michalowska and John Bingham-Hall
58	Contributors
60	Acknowledgements

Introduction

John Bingham-Hall   I think one of the tensions for us about this reframing of the organisation as an institution is the proximity between doing and reflecting. What do we mean by the word institution? Everyone within the organisation is a maker of some kind: doing writing, doing research, doing sound editing, making creative work. But we're also hosts, and hosting is a really complicated practice to get right. We've learned that the hard way through mistakes in hosting in other institutional contexts. It is difficult to do both: make the work and be the host; be the voice and the platform.

So, does the institution always need to be only the host? If you have an institution where the members of it are also its voices and performers, could that lead to solidarities between artists and institutions? What happens when there's not a clear division between those positions? Would an artist we invite into the organisation then work together as a peer with the organisation?

Susannah Haslam   I love the idea that becoming an institution might be resolved through thinking about what hosting means. Hosting in a careful and caring sense is when we think about people: the who of the institution, the identities, the bodies of the institution, and the necessary systems of care around them. Hosting is also about being propped up by supporting structures, which is often what we talk about in relation to infrastructure. So, it's at once a form of kinship and intimacy, and the manifestation of four walls, or a space, that is defined by its material institutional qualities.

John Bingham-Hall   I think one of the problems with big institutions is that the people working within them are not valorised as their creative selves as much as they should be. And so, maybe those solidarities can come from institutions acknowledging that they are a set of voices already, before they look at which voices they even invite in.

Often we only become aware of infrastructure when it is broken. The *when* of infrastructure implies a degree of relational thinking: what leads to infrastructure, and how is it made visible? When infrastructure's functioning is broken, as users, protagonists, friends, interlocutors, we become inconvenienced, required to find an alternative way to travel, to consume, to rest, to socialise, to acknowledge that, for many in urban contexts, this corruption marks a seam, or an edge, in an otherwise seamless, or edgeless, cultural life. It may not be difficult to imagine: a road with traffic cones, amber lights flashing, where your time and navigational capacities are subjected to someone else's; being put on hold, met with endless loops of pre-recorded information when trying to make an appointment with a GP, while the urgency of your call is at odds with the urgency of everyone else's; the razing of repurposed enclaves of fun (carparks, railway arches, parks) in cities to image someone else's idea of community, where communities are then priced out; the price of an exhibition ticket making it impossible to visit until the end of the month (if at all); the cost of a university degree being outrageously disproportionate to the paper granted at the end of it; and means of accessing resourcing options for the above are often the reserve of those who are already within it. Countless further examples could be listed here to highlight how infrastructure becomes visible when it is broken, challenged, or when its functions privilege one group of people over others, or exclude certain ideas, or behaviours, in favour of an ideal usership, or use. How does this apply to cultural infrastructure? What needs to break for a city's cultural infrastructure to become visible? And how can this break function to better support and sustain existing cultural infrastructure to make it more accessible and more equally distributed?

The relationships between cities and cultures that entwine to form public life are complex: visible yet hidden, functional yet fallible, meaningful, disconnected, precarious, alive. These relationships underpin Theatrum Mundi's *Making Cultural Infrastructure* project, which uses the lens of stagecraft – the set of crafts that need to come together to stage a production, both onstage and backstage – to look at public life in cities. This perspective locates the *performance* of city life and culture at the centre of Theatrum Mundi's enquiry into cultural infrastructure, while asking whether the infrastructural conditions for culture can be designed into a city. Another way to approach this enquiry into cultural infrastructure is to consider the *existing* conditions that already *make* cultural infrastructure in cities. Those conditions might be best understood as environments, settings, backgrounds and contexts *for* culture. They can be referred to as *infrastructures* and function to materialise and organise cultural production. Infrastructural conditions are varied and shapeshifting: they are at once affective – influencing, or shaping, actions or behaviours, or making people feel a certain way; and they are also highly pragmatic and functional protocols – cold, edged, material. In urban contexts, cultural infrastructure might be commonly recognised as the structural and symbolic armatures that stage what constitutes culture: museums, theatres, art galleries, libraries, music venues. More specifically, one might also imagine some of the smaller-scale or less generally known spaces that support cultural activity: specialist archives that demonstrate multitudinous histories; artist studios that make communities; kitchens that manifest long-held recipes for hosting and eating delicious food; dance floors that enable bodies to move freely together; and workspaces, in and out of domestic environments. Alongside, there are some mutable, perhaps accidental, infrastructures that provide the setting for many different activities to take place, such as the concrete promenade of London's Southbank: the Southbank Centre and Southbank skatepark, as two planes of the same infrastructure, one above the ground, the other below that same ground.

Visibility and invisibility play a key role in understanding and accessing the conditions that support cultural infrastructure; where ground is less of a limit, and more membrane. Yet, the conditions that support these places and activities are often configured *elsewhere*, or are subject to someone else's idea of what those places and activities should be through, for example, policy-making at the Department for Digital, Culture, Media and Sport, or public funding bodies, such as Arts Council England, or charities such as Create London. These bodies set some of the conditions that make cultural infrastructure, and thus make culture happen, in theory.

To ask how existing infrastructural conditions that support cultural production in cities can be better supported and sustained, made more accessible, and more equally distributed, is a question that requires the perspective of makers of culture – producers and organisers – as a starting point. It is also a question of *who*, *when*, and *where*: who defines what cultural infrastructure is; when and where does it happen?

Cultural theorist Lauren Berlant proposes that infrastructure is 'the living mediation that organises life',[1] and 'that which binds us to the world in movement and keeps the world practically bound to itself',[2] and so it is something that *lives* and *organises* concurrently, and is active, not passive, mutable, not static. Berlant's thinking on infrastructure also concerns a glitch or break. Curator and writer Legacy Russell talks about the glitch: that which gives primacy to the state, event, or condition of the glitched *thing*, rather than the perceived smooth normalcy that is broken by it. For Russell, the glitch is the habitus of contemporary radical feminism, a point of access to thinking how identities are shaped through technological irregularity, or *mal*function, both at and away from the keyboard – especially for those that 'embrace the causality of error [...] this glitch is a correction to the "machine"'. The glitch is lived with and by and through. In their work, Berlant and Russell pose this type of *infrastructural thinking* as ways to recognise fallible social(ised) patterns, behaviours, or textures of lives, which can, at any point, become critically disrupted or perforated.

To demonstrate a range of points at which this disruption or perforation might occur, and their affects and effects, one can imagine activity both at and away from the keyboard: the use of ever-new and nuanced visual languages in the circulation of memes; the practise of posting storied images on social media to perform participation in cultural and social life; hacking into the infrastructure of cultural institutions; unbuilding institutions (and buildings) to expose what can otherwise be seen or known. For example, memeclasseworldwide is an artist group based in Kiel, Germany, who, while at Muthesius Kunsthochschule, intervened in their own art school curriculum by setting up an informal *weisungsfreie klasse* to discuss and materialise meme culture in free classrooms and via an Instagram account (all the while asking whether art school had missed out on the Internet). Instead of asking whether art school should do more *with* or *on* the Internet, as social communication infrastructure, the group proposed that the intervening curriculum should function to 'find entry into the mutation of languages in images, text, and aesthetic and political discourses that originate on the web'[3] in order to bring those mutations back into the art school as critical matter.

In her work *Excellence and Perfections* (2014), artist Amalia Ulman performs a life in parts on Instagram and Facebook, involving a slow reveal/construct of semi-fictional scenarios that Ulman has composed. For users of social media, it is not new that feeds and stories are ways of conceiving of and constructing personal images and imaginaries: 'Ulman went to great lengths to replicate the narrative conventions of [them] from her use of captions and hashtags [...] to the pace and

---

1   Berlant, L. (2016) 'The commons: Infrastructures for troubling times'. *Society and Space*, 34(3): p. 393.
2   Ibid. p. 394.

3   Garnicnig, B. (2021) 'Has art school missed out on the internet?', *Art & Education* [https://www.artandeducation.net/classroom/413615/memeclassworldwide/]

timing of uploads, to the discerning inclusion of "authentic" intimate or emotional content.'[4] Ulman, in a similar way to the memeclassworldwide's intervention in the curriculum, uses methods of puncture and disruption to open the *critical* possibility of breaking the smooth infrastructure of social life on Instagram.

Infrastructure commonly relies on the binary of breaking and subsequent fixing or replacement or embellishment, which operates between ontologies and appears benign while being otherwise. For Berlant, it is in a novel approach to the *fixing of*, or attending to, the broken that infrastructure's radical capacities emerge. A poignant example of this *fixing* is artist Tania Bruguera's working group called Tate Neighbours, formed as part of her 2018-19 Hyundai commission for Tate Modern titled *10, 148, 451*. Bruguera invited residents of the London Borough of Southwark *into* the infrastructure, as well as the institution, to work *with* the institution. Among many interventions, Tate Neighbours have notably – permanently – changed the name of the Boiler House Building at Tate Modern to the Natalie Bell Building, after activist Natalie Bell who plays an instrumental role in grassroots community leadership with young people in Southwark. This act of *breaking into* an otherwise highly controlled bureaucratic framework – the renaming of a building, which is usually awarded in return for significant financial patronage – is remarkable, and throws into sharp relief the system – and the systemic make-up – of a cultural institution.

These forms of infrastructural intervention can be paralleled by what queer theorist Jack Halberstam proposes through the infrastructural practice of *unbuilding*. Halberstam illustrates the notion of *unbuilding gender* with artist Gordon Matta-Clark's *anarchitecture* practice: specifically, works such as *Splitting* (1974) and *Day's End* (1975) throw light and cast shadows, inside and outside of cut-into buildings, a house and a warehouse, to demonstrate the 'refusal of certain political paradigms for the urban environment',[5] that is, assumed coherence between bodies and sites, and the vulnerabilities and brutalities presented by the incoherence of cut-into buildings. As a cultural and linguistic institution that limits, and defines and holds power, gender is something to be unbuilt. Halberstam describes the critical possibilities of unbuilding what is known, commonly, in order to reveal what can be seen, otherwise. Matta-Clark introduces splits and cuts into buildings – anarchitecture – which serves to (re)produce or speculate on the not-quite-there, already-gone essence of a building, its potential and its transience in forming (non)gendered spatio-cultural narratives of a city.

The research that informs this publication, developed as part of my fellowship at Theatrum Mundi, has explored parts of the relationship between cultural institutions and cultural infrastructures, specifically by asking how cultural practitioners and organisers can work with the existing infrastructural conditions of cultural institutions. Taking Tania Bruguera's work at Tate Modern in 2018 and 2019 as a starting point and building on her methods of infrastructural *arrest*, *intervention* and *co-option*, this research has looked at cultural infrastructure through active, existing practices of infrastructure in London. It has been important to locate practices, and practitioners, that do – rather than diagnose – the what and when of

---

[4] *Amalia Ulman: Excellences and Perfections* (n.d.) [https://www.newmuseum.org/exhibitions/view/amalia-ulman-excellences-perfections]

[5] Halberstam, J. (2018), 'Unbuilding Gender', *Places Journal* [https://placesjournal.org/article/unbuilding-gender/#0]

infrastructure. To this end, *infrastructuring* is understood as the practice of intervening into existing cultural infrastructure. This Edition brings together four dialogues with cultural practitioners and organisers based in London, conducted throughout 2020, in an attempt to consider the type of *infrastructuring*, or *infrastructural* practice, that goes beyond doorways and buildings and signs and language. Each of the edited conversations offers a perspective of and on *practising infrastructurally* at cross-sections of London's cultural landscape: art, hospitality, education, advocacy, heritage, museums, urbanism and research, from the vantage point of the personal, affective and transformative qualities of infrastructure. Collectively, they demonstrate the critical breadth and depth, reflexivity, detail, poetics, struggle, commitment, love and tireless work of cities' cultural infrastructure.

Artist and activist Sean Roy Parker works across cultural forms, consolidating a making and facilitation practice between art and hospitality. We first spoke in the summer of 2020 to discuss the processes and conditions by and on which the maxims *doing it yourself* (DIY), *doing it together* (DIT) and *doing it with others* (DIWO) are made possible in an increasingly difficult urban context bound to financialised public/private paradigms. Curator, educator, agitator and resource builder Cecilia Wee speaks from a position of action. We also spoke during the summer of 2020 to discuss the *inside* and *outside* of cultural institutional practice, Cecilia's work in service of justice and change, the types of relationships that exist *between* individuals within the cultural sphere, the systems that exist *within* the cultural sphere, and the prospect of unbuilding cultural institutions. Curator of contemporary programmes at the Victoria and Albert Museum in London, Meneesha Kellay speaks about her encounters with cultural infrastructures across the public, private and charity sectors, as a programmer, curator and organiser. We spoke during the autumn of 2020 to discuss what it means to practise infrastructurally, as a critical, responsible and accountable approach to working within institutions. Co-directors of Theatrum Mundi, Marta Michalowska and John Bingham-Hall, give voice to an organisation resisting institutionalisation. We spoke during the winter of 2020 to discuss what it means to be a small-scale research organisation, the challenges such organisations face to work ethically, equitably and responsibly, what valuable contribution to culture is, and how it can be practised by the organisation at every level.

One
○ Amateurship as resistance
○ Natural and artificial surplus
○ Repurposing found materials
○ Redistributing knowledge

Two
○ Being in service to justice and change
○ People as infrastructure
○ Failing institutions
○ Interlocutors with systems

Three
○ MASS Action
○ Ownership of Culture
○ Public service
○ Understanding vs Performance

Four
○ Putting solidarities to work
○ Risk and responsibility
○ Reorganisation
○ Artistic production vs Experience

Doing It Yourself/Together/With Others (DIY/T/WO)

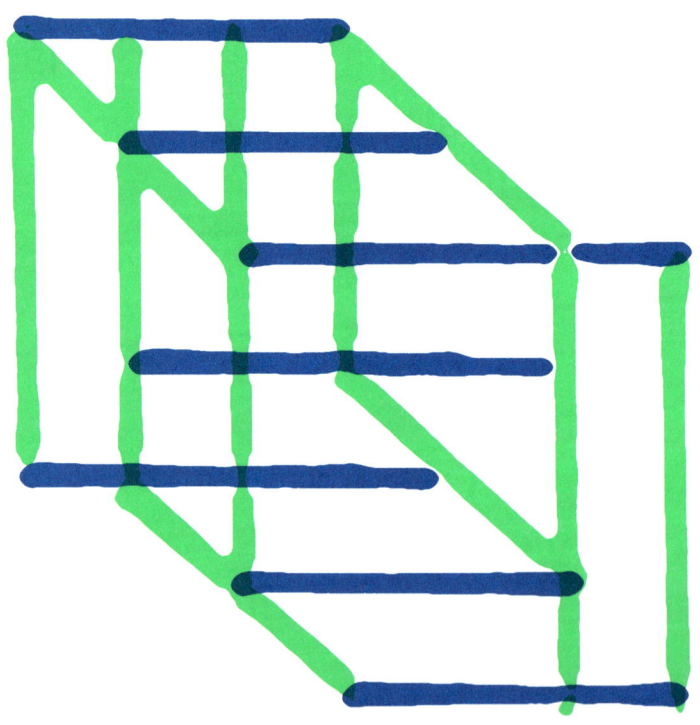

A conversation with Sean Roy Parker [SRP]
Tuesday, 16 June 2020. Glengall Wharf Garden, London

Sean Roy Parker is a UK-based, eco-anxious artist, environmentalist and fermenter. Sean Roy lives and works by the values of amateurism, skill-sharing and building alternative work models. His practice is infrastructural: constructing frameworks for and facilitating collaboration. We met to talk at Glengall Wharf Garden in north Peckham, London, a volunteer-led community garden that lies on the edge of Burgess Park to the west and the Surrey Canal Path to the south. At the time, Sean Roy was volunteering at Glengall Wharf and had previously led workshops and tours from the garden. I wanted to speak with Sean Roy about his movement between self-organised and Doing It Yourself/Together/With Others (DIY/T/WO) work; the balance his practice strikes between art and food and organisation; the principles of sustainability, equity, and responsibility which frame his practice and thinking and form a vital component of cultural infrastructure in urban settings. Self-organisation and DIY/T/WO practices are often invisible, like infrastructure, despite being premised on action, or change, but unlike infrastructure, processes of disbanding or breaking are part of their life cycle, often replaced or subject to evolution.

○ Abundance
○ Artificial surplus
○ Autonomy
○ Foraging
○ Found materials
○ Natural surplus

SH   As a starting point to our conversation, please tell me what you do.

SRP   I always get nervous when someone asks me what I do. I call myself *an eco-anxious visual artist and cook*; you could also interpret my work as environmental activism.

     I work with found materials and explore their life cycles, particularly thinking about how I relate to being in the city with natural and artificial surplus, empty spaces, free time. I try to create frameworks within which to explore the post-capital ideas of redistributing knowledge, abundance and care. These take a lot of different forms. For example, I work with under-represented demographics, especially disabled and neurodiverse communities. I've done a lot of volunteering at a charity called Action Space, which works with disabled artists in a supported studio setting. And I've also been an employment coach, supporting Learning Disabled and Autistic people into paid work. These experiences have had a huge impact on the way I see myself as a cultural producer: the ways I use my voice and my presence, and I absorb or deflect materials and thoughts.

     My practice is a scaffold for thinking about immaterial labour within institutions, for trying to unfold and unpick the, often oppressive, hierarchies in the art world and non-art worlds of food, labour or travel. I've come from a hospitality background, and a lot of my work since has been dedicated to challenging that singular voice of financialised business models, exploring non-traditional models and alternative currencies.

     My work is also about the privatisation of green space, so I spend time outside, in what we might call nature, but what is a man-made artifice, and try to help people connect with outdoor spaces as one of the last bastions of the city where you don't have to spend money but time instead. For example, through workshops, foraging, scavenging, wildflower identification and litter picking, I encourage people to think how our bodies fit in with the environment, and how that can lead to critical thinking around mental wellbeing and collaboration.

SH   How do you see those practices connect, or not, with the existing cultural infrastructure of the city? Do you see the work you do as providing cultural infrastructure?

SRP   I'm trying to confront some really obvious injustices, using art as the tool and creative thinking as the methodology, rather than the outcome. In the past, as an artist with *traditional* training, I would undertake a publishing project, and the book would be the output, or I'd make sculptures, and an exhibition would be the output. And I got to a point where I didn't think that was fulfilling a deeper purpose, a deeper meaning, and didn't know what the essence of my practice was. I knew that I had to transcend the narrow, prescribed idea of what an artist should be doing to find a medium that allowed me to combine self-expression and social function. At its heart, my work is about widening access – physical, financial, social, mental, spiritual.

SH   You have moved from the idea of contributing objects to existing cultural infrastructure to *enabling* alternative cultural infrastructure. This seems to be a practice of mediation, or facilitation, at many different thresholds of art and hospitality, for example. These thresholds provide access: moments or points to move through and engage with those injustices within art and hospitality.
I really enjoyed reading your interview with Olivia Dreisinger in *ECO-CRIPS*, which discussed your work and its use of material resources; the complexities of civic responsibility around food and surplus food; collaborative problem-solving; and the associated economies of action your work inspires. Can you say a bit more about what has led you to this point?

SRP   My work is very much about access, but it's also about identifying weaknesses: the obvious frailties of the capitalist system that oppresses the working classes and marginalised voices. But first and foremost, my practice is about finding what I like to do and mutating that into something that can be shared or applied. I spent a long time in my twenties concerning myself with being validated by peers, which is a rite of passage for many. It meant that I was always aiming to have my work exhibited, and I wanted to be noticed. As I became more aware that I sat on the outside of the mainstream – and that was actually a good place for me to be – I could partake in the art world socially and enjoy what was happening inside, but I didn't really see how these artists were getting paid or how they were sustaining their lifestyle. Essentially, the desire to put an artwork into an exhibition that had no financial benefit was built on social capital. A lot of artists were also working in disgusting and violent workplaces. I'm thinking here particularly about hospitality, where the single voice and imperative of financial gain is often unchallenged.

SH   Could you talk about some of the projects that define this shift in your practice.

SRP   In 2009, I met a few people who studied at Goldsmiths, and they were starting a poetry collective called Clinic, which developed from meeting up in the Marquis of Granby, in New Cross, London. They came up with the name when getting a check-up at the sexual health clinic, and they decided that they wanted to put on a poetry reading in the Amersham Arms, also in New Cross. They wanted to make a pamphlet of their writing and asked me to design it. I didn't know what I was doing, but I was training to be a graphic designer and really wanted them to like me, so I just did it. We photocopied it in my room, collaged it all together, photocopied it, and then I stapled it using a regular stapler and a courgette, because I didn't have a long-arm stapler, so the finished pamphlets had green stains around the bind.

We wanted to do a launch, but we knew that just doing a poetry reading was going to have no impact at all; there were no poetry nights in South London that we knew of. So we also booked bands that we knew, mostly obscure math rock bands, and put on an exhibition of local artists. It was a kind of club night that we self-funded while we were studying. It was a very ramshackle operation, my first experience of DIY.

We published some amazing books that I'm proud of, even the bad ones, because we did it totally ourselves. Clinic was so passionate about different voices in poetry and so absolutely hellbent on producing beautiful publications that weren't stuffy. We tried different visual approaches: full colour art inserts, flipping poems on their side across double spreads, and one design had pages alternating in purple and teal ink. And I felt really energised by this, the fact that we were making the decisions autonomously. A couple of the pamphlets that we produced won the London Review of Books' Pamphlet of the Year: Chloe Stopa-Hunt's *White Hills* and Rebecca Tamás's *Savage*. We would go and represent ourselves at book fairs and curate reading events. I would go as far as to say – without having been a poet myself, but having viewed it from inside and outside – that we went some way to laying the foundations for what is now quite a healthy poetry landscape in London in terms of reading, representation and format.

SH   You were cheered on by a wider context of other people doing similar things, engaging with, as you mentioned, a form of DIY cultural practice. DIY is very much about responding to a singular moment, and it is also often about resisting being held by one voice, one idea, or one way of practising, which I think is important in terms of how your work has evolved.

SRP   Yes, and through writing our own rule book, and through manifesting our desires for what we wanted to see in poetry, Clinic ended up being quite coveted. We were always invited to do book launches and collaborative readings at art spaces like Hannah Barry Gallery, moving poetry into where it wasn't really expected. It was simultaneously bringing poetry friends into new spaces and exposing new audiences to a range of poetry. When programming, we'd have serious poets, and then we'd have a really funny poet. We'd chop it all up, so that we knew that there would be potentially something for everyone. I think we can look back on Clinic in years to come and maybe someone will write something about it. I feel like it was important at that time, in the early 2010s.

SH   So what came after Clinic?

SRP   In 2013, I took an evening pottery course with a friend, fell in love with it straight away and started building my own plant pots, beakers and soap dishes. I was trying to kit my flat out. After a few years of messing around in my studio and some nice commissions, I started working as a studio apprentice at Kiln Rooms in Peckham. Although I didn't like it much, I stuck with it as I could use their space and materials for free in return.

I noticed the sink traps – the boxes under the sinks where solids would settle and clean water would run off – were always full of sludge: different clays, glazes, oxides, dust, staples. I would scoop that out and take it in a big bin back to my studio. I upset some studio members as it smelled bad – what can I say? I'm attracted to free stuff and amorphous media.

Deciding how I could utilise waste materials became a challenge, a methodology. The output was constrained by these materials that had already had a history. The ceramics were so sloppy and weird that I had to be really stubborn with it. I got really caught up in the beauty of the found materials without too much critical rigour.

This was slightly before the national revival of ceramics, signified by The Great Pottery Throwdown, but immediately succeeding the cancellation of craft courses in large institutions, which produced many highly-influential potters over the years, including Grayson Perry. I remember Camberwell College of Arts cancelled their ceramics courses and sold, or donated, all their equipment to smaller regional colleges. Then, the following year, ceramics became wildly popular again, so they had shot themselves in the foot, and everyone wondered why they'd done it. Personally, I feel this epitomises the homogenisation of creative education in the neoliberal austerity agenda.

SH   It also seemed to be the time for you to find your discipline in terms of not only the material practice and the ceramics that you were making and the repurposing of used materials, but also the ethics: the practice very much situated in the context of what you had access to, what you didn't have access to, and how you could manoeuvre that. There's something really interesting in how this period between Clinic and the ceramics studio is the formation of your own discipline: you are constructing systems, mechanics, materials and limitations. What happened next?

SRP   After four years, I was fed up with my job in hospitality. I was spending more and more time at work, overworking my body, drinking too much and trying desperately to please everyone. I just got sick of it and figured the only way that I could break the cycle was to move away. I convinced my partner at the time that we should move to the seaside. In 2016, I left my studio, my flat and my job, and I thought I could just have a clean break and go to the seaside. It was an amazing move. It set the tone for risk-taking – the idea of giving up things that are comfortable for the pursuit of something that is unknown – and I became almost unafraid of failing. I had very little to lose.

When I moved to Hastings, I didn't really have a job, so I was money-poor but time-rich, and this flipped my value system. I turned up to this amazing, beautiful landscape that I hadn't really spent time in since I was a child. I had the freedom of knowing that – because my rent was cheap – I only had to make x amount of money, and the rest of the time, I could spend outside. I decided against getting a studio and bought a small *Observer Book of Wildflowers* for £2 off eBay. I would walk to Bexhill or cycle to Eastbourne, identifying all the plants along the way. Because I have a very short attention span, I very quickly moved on to thinking about traditional uses of wild plants in cooking, medicine and building. At that time, I wasn't thinking about it as *art*. It was a bit of exercise or some outdoor therapy.

SH   While in Hastings, you got accepted onto the alternative, nomadic, anti-institutional-memory MFA programme, School of the Damned. What spurred this decision, and how did this experience consolidate your work to this point?

SRP   I was attracted by the idea that I would get to travel around the country with School of the Damned. I was enamoured by the idea of meeting new people and forming decentralised friendships because I felt my experience of the arts community in London had been narrow and often controlled by cultural gatekeepers. In School of the Damned, we lived in disparate locations. We weren't very ethnically diverse but were mostly working class and genderqueer. We would soon learn how democratic decision-making propelled the project: there were no tutors, and there was no physical home, so it was really a baptism of fire.

The way that the school resisted institutionalisation through respawning every year meant that we were able to make the same mistakes as probably the five previous years had made. And I think that's very important in a project that was originally designed as a political stand against the privatisation and the financialisation of universities. No institutional memory, just a legacy; all we got was an email address and a couple of contacts in the art world that we might want to contact for a workshop, and a logo.

It's fascinating to build something up from the ground with a group of people that you've never met, with aims that you're not even sure about. And then you have a few people that take the lead, and you realise that there's space and time for everyone. It's about friendship, it's about care, it's about support.

It really clarified to me that my practice and the energy – the love that I get from making art – is in collaboration, in unknown spaces between people, in the convergence.

SH   These encounters with self-organisation and collaborative working prompted you to set up PEFA …

SRP   My dad used to say, 'What's the dog's name? It's Defa, D for dog.' So, I came up with PEFA: P for projects, and some supporting acronyms: Preserve Environment For All; Protect Education From Austerity; Politically Engage Fringe Artists.

When I came up with PEFA, I was thinking how I was going to infiltrate art institutions, how I was going to develop public programming skills, how I was going to work with people to share knowledge, skills and ideas. Removing my own name – as an artist – seemed to be the most appropriate way to do that. This way, PEFA is also slightly separate from my visual art practice.

In summer 2017, I was invited to do something with the Towner Gallery in Eastbourne. I said, 'Hey, shall we go and identify wildflowers on the beach and litter pick?' Rather than thinking about obvious outcomes such as an exhibition or a public programme, I was hovering around the idea of workshop as an artistic medium, workshop as methodology.

PEFA was a manifestation of the aspects of public programming that I felt were missing in institutions. Having not been involved or invited into a lot of institutions before, I was really trying to act on a feeling that there was a distinct absence of any public programming that promoted skill-sharing.

Then, in spring 2018, I was commissioned to present a workshop at Tate Britain and, beyond working with a great staff member, found the whole experience pretty frustrating. The public programmes seemed to be assembled by people who were working in admin-heavy jobs, producing fairly unimaginative outcomes with very famous artists. Although you would imagine event curation as expansive and dynamic, the outcomes were tightly controlled in order to fulfil predetermined metrics, which meant I didn't have much freedom in my proposal and ended up feeling like I was ticking a box.

The uptake was poor, even though it was a free workshop with a long lead time and good promotion. It made me question how Tate Britain created relationships with their neighbours, and whether it extended beyond money going through the till. It made me think about the local responsibility of an institution, and whether its impenetrable bureaucracy blocked opportunities to make meaningful connections with patrons, visitors and collaborators.

SH   You wanted to intervene in that outcome-based setup in arts institutions by producing workshops as an artistic medium and methodology, so producing became your skillset. Alongside PEFA, you started to work at the Brixton Pound Cafe, making a leap back to hospitality.

SRP   When I moved back to London after eighteen months in Hastings, I was in Brixton and walked into the Brixton Pound Cafe, a community cafe, which was chaotic in a charming way. I took on a couple of days' work in the kitchen under an amazing Polish vegan chef, Iga, who taught me so much about preparation, service and preservation. After a few months, I took over the day-to-day running of the project, and while very stressful, it was formative in my development. Creative thinking became a way of problem-solving rather than an aesthetic output. I was able to apply my practice to a real-life model.

The Brixton Pound Cafe was at the time one of London's only pay-what-you-can food projects. We accepted donations of surplus food intercepted before landfill by charities FareShare and City Harvest, turning it into healthy, affordable vegetarian and vegan lunches. I saw working there as an opportunity to combine my hospitality experience, as a manager of people and staff, with my interest in collaboration. And there was also a connection to the found materials, but this time in the form of food.

The first thing I did when I got the job was to question the existing *pay-as-you-feel* model, which asks people to make a value judgement. And this was in Brixton, one of the trendiest food spots in London, at the very time when it was becoming gentrified. It felt tokenistic, as if we were asking for charity. I thought that was a submissive position for the business to put itself in, but replacing *what-you-feel* with *what-you-can* instigated conversations around privilege and access: 'it costs this much' becomes 'what can you afford?' In an area with high deprivation and food insecurity, we wanted to make sure that everyone could use the cafe and eat our food, while drawing attention to income inequality.

At the Brixton Pound Cafe, I had the freedom to bring together a small team of people with different interests in a co-op style organisation. We earned the same regardless of our roles. I felt it was important to flatten the hierarchy and share responsibility for the project horizontally. I wanted to work with multiple voices to create something that benefited the participants, and to recruit volunteers who were friendly, enthusiastic and interested in fighting food waste. The cafe was very fortunate to have input from many incredible individuals from marginalised backgrounds, including underemployed, Black, Indigenous People of Colour, LGBTQI elders, and those with mental health issues. We also worked with a local school to provide supported volunteering opportunities for students with Learning Disabilities and Autism.

SH   As an inherited project, the Brixton Pound Cafe carries with it a history in terms of alternative economic practice. I'm thinking here of the use of a local, alternative currency, and to me this is a political act. I'm curious to hear how you think the decentralised processes you established there could evolve to shape cultural practices in other urban contexts? Perhaps you could talk about it in relation to art, education and food. The work you were doing at the Brixton Pound Cafe seems to have compounded your practice.

SRP   Yes, I would say that at the Brixton Pound Cafe a compounding of a plethora of interests, concerns, and testing out how they might work in a non-financialised business structure have taken place. The board of directors of the cafe were not prescriptive about how they wanted me to run it. I had autonomy with the project as long as I returned enough money for them to pay the rent.

Alongside the daily cafe, we had to come up with inventive ways of bringing in money to cover our wages and the rent. At one point, we were hiring out the basement four nights a week for parties, running supper clubs and workshops out-of-hours upstairs, and providing catering for local events. It was wild, and I definitely burnt out!

I think with the Brixton Pound Cafe, what I was trying to do was to push the model literally to the edge of where it could go without imploding. And I feel that the School of the Damned was the same, in a way, it was held together with hope and gaffer tape. It was an embodiment of a radical concept, lived out through a series of temporary exchanges and events. Running the Brixton Pound Cafe was my way of pushing something as far as possible with meagre resources: very limited cash and very limited expertise. It embodied the stubborn, visceral amateurship that I defend so much in my practice. I would say that amateurship forms a resistance to over-professionalisation. It's a big part of my identity, and so it feeds into my work.

Living, creating art, being a cultural producer, and fulfilling other people's expectations, is pandering to other people's needs. In a way, it's about giving them the nice thing at the end, and that in itself erases a lot of the actual, emotional and physical labour, it erases a lot of the mental work, it erases all the acrobatics that go into it, in the same way that hospitality does.

SH   Absolutely, and those frames of reference in cultural institutions and hospitality you have mentioned often co-opt what is on their edges: this is usually referred to as box-ticking, without any real, sustainable work dedicated to inclusivity and equitability. So in amateurship, perhaps, there's an element of resistance to that co-option. Could you give other examples of everyday actions of resistance?

SRP   It's a difficult question because I am extremely privileged in many ways, so I can make choices that I know a lot of my contemporaries aren't able to make, whether it's about work, time, education or food. I've thought about it a lot, and it seems that, in terms of food, the responsibility for ethical consumption has been lumped on an individual. For example, you should stop buying that stuff in plastic. Why are you buying the apples in plastic?

I think this is deeply unfair because you might not have the luxury of time, money or variety. The shop you may want to go to may be inaccessible. This assignment of responsibility to an individual is accusatory and distracting. The decisions of an individual are being weaponised, and we are blaming each other for systemic problems when, in fact, we should be asking: why are the apples in plastic in the first place; where do the apples come from; why is food being imported from a different country when we're perfectly good at growing it here? I'm trying to think about how to re-localise and redistribute seasonal resources. Decarbonisation of art is my motivation, and the question is always the answer: global climate crisis is a class struggle, a race struggle, a capitalist struggle. I think we're finding out that it is also a feminist struggle.

SH During the day of discussions I was involved in organising with John Bingham-Hall from Theatrum Mundi and Tram Nguyen and Annie Bicknell from Tate Modern, as part of *Talking as Neighbours* at Tate Exchange in February 2019, artist Tash Cox and curator Eva Rowson led a panel on what can be done within cultural institutions daily to ensure that different voices are heard, so that the labour undertaken at every point in the institution, at an infrastructural level, is acknowledged, especially in predominantly public-facing contexts. Eva asked, 'Who does the washing-up?', as a way of highlighting structural inequalities of visible and invisible labour.

SRP You seem to be talking about allyship. There is a lot of work to be done to challenge structural and systemic violence that occurs as a result of the invisibility of labour in cultural institutions, of not acknowledging the labour inequalities. I would like to refer back to Eva's question with emphasis on the *who*: '*Who* does the washing-up?'

As white people, we've let violence happen, and we've been complicit in our silence. And so, what I feel like I'm trying to do is to use my privilege to infiltrate the systems – the ordinary systems – and regulate or decarbonise or decolonise them in a way that is very particular to me. It's not necessarily the purest form, but it's my interpretation of how I can use my stubbornness, my passion, my skills, to create better frameworks for sustainable practice. Ultimately, a lot of what I do is creating frameworks to invite multitudes of voices and create complex multi-layered narratives that I have very little control over or input into.

SH Yes, decentralising as well as decarbonising and decolonising tired and exclusionary mechanisms of cultural institutions. Before, you mentioned that Camberwell College of Arts closed its craft courses and began redistributing resources and industrial equipment. This is strangely one version of what you're saying.

SRP Yes, it's disassembling the city in a way, and I'm really interested in that idea. I've written 'abolish' and circled it in my notes. That's a hot term at the moment, and something that I do genuinely believe could be a way forward in terms of cultural institutions – defunding them and redistributing their resources. I think decentralising access to materials, skills and knowledge is a way to disempower the singularity of the city, and institutions within it, as a cultural hub.

I also want to mention the competition of the everyday. Capitalist careerism is one of the most debilitating things that I can think of, and it permeates every aspect of my practice. Collaboration and cooperation are the absolute opposite of it, and can take many different working forms. The School of the Damned was one of those alternatives.

So how do we formulate frameworks with people and communities who are outside of the narrow understanding of (predominantly visual) culture? How do we create frameworks for subsistence and empowerment? We look at everything through a white, able-bodied, colonial gaze, and this perpetuates the intended audience forever. It all comes down to money and commerce at the end of the day, so the whole idea of high-profile museums and galleries posturing as cultural institutions is kind of a lie, isn't it? In reality, they are shady, financialised corporations with aesthetic facades. We're only concerned with who the Tate is exhibiting because we're listening to a very, very, very small amount of people's viewpoints about what they believe will be popular. And we know it's mostly white, dead males who have blockbuster shows. So *why* is it relevant? I don't know. Maybe this is the question to end on: but why is it relevant? And in what ways do institutions convince those who are under-represented to work harder and continue to wait patiently to be validated by a system that will never respect them?

SH Or how can artists move the mirror to shift what it is reflecting?

SRP Essentially, an institution is a memory bank, right? And it keeps on saying that only a sliver of all history is worth remembering. For me, the ultimate purpose of art is to be a collaborative tool. It's a way of processing trauma. It is a way of expressing yourself. It's a way of being in touch with yourself in an anti-capitalist way. That's just my interpretation, and it keeps me sane.

Breaking Cultural Infrastructure

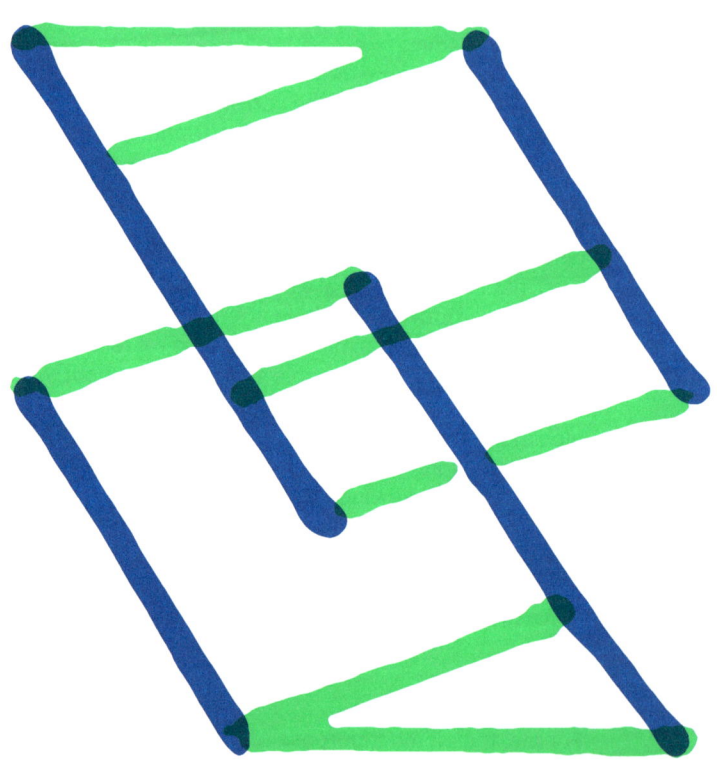

A conversation with Cecilia Wee [CW]
Tuesday, 7 July 2020. SquadCast, online platform, London

Cecilia Wee is a London-based curator, educator, agitator and resource builder. Cecilia works inside and outside of cultural and educational institutions and organisations, advisory and governance boards and committees in the arts, and runs her own imprint and agency tdwm – *ting dao wo ma?* (Mandarin Chinese for 'can you hear me?') Cecilia's work addresses the (in)visibilities in the cultural and education sectors that are the result of inequitable, precarious practice and infrastructure for art and social action. We met to talk online while we were working from our respective homes in South London, mid-pandemic. I wanted to speak with Cecilia about her work in and out of cultural and educational institutions. How have her encounters in and out of institutions led her to find a combined, dexterous practice of activism, curating, educating and research? How do these experiences shape her public work in writing, curating, programming, broadcasting and teaching? And what does it mean to be an agitator in the cultural sector in the UK?

○ Grassroots
○ Interrogating
○ In/visibility

○ In support
○ Probing
○ Unpicking

SH   Could you tell me a little bit more about what you do, and what is cultural infrastructure in relation to that?

CW   I describe myself as a curator, researcher, educator and cultural agitator. I think it's important to preface what I do by acknowledging that politics is very much part of what I do. I used to make radio programmes about contemporary art and culture on Resonance FM; I have edited books, curated exhibitions, events, and all sorts of projects, working with experimental performance and music, with different types of visual art and design practices. And what I do is always in service to justice and change; it's always in service to unpicking, probing, and interrogating the types of relationships that exist between individuals within the cultural sphere, and the systems that exist within cultural institutions. I'm doing work in support of those individuals, or those communities, who have been marginalised and underserved in those contexts.

    I was chair of the Live Art Development Agency (LADA), and I've been involved in boards and governance. I was on the Arts Council England's (ACE) London Area Council from 2008 to 2014, which means that I experienced the arc of policy shifts from the so-called heydays, before the global financial crisis, through the financial crash period in 2008, the London Olympics in 2012, and then the restructuring of ACE's regular funding in the first National Portfolio Organisation funding round for 2015-18, which was a big reorganisation of what arts funding could be, and what it means to the people applying for it.

    The work that I do now is increasingly grassroots, which, in a sense, is a counter-trajectory to the one that you might imagine as you get older. I was doing policy work and being called to speak within those more abstract circles, and now I try to do the frontline work, and I try to make sense of what it means to do that work, even though it's not very visible.

    The reason why I say all this is because this idea of visibility is really important to the question of infrastructure. Infrastructures become visible when they break down, or when they are challenged. Suddenly there's an instability that makes you question the strength of bonds, and those bonds might be personal, or they might be institutional and organisational.

    A lot of the things that people are dealing with now, particularly during a pandemic, are about the blurred lines between life, work and play. This is also wrapped up with our understanding of a choice made in the pursuit of a creative life, which brings to mind Giorgio Vasari's *The Lives of the Most Excellent Painters, Sculptors, and Architects*, from 1550, which was so crucial to European ideas of artistic canons, individual genius and artists as celebrities. In other words, politically, what does it mean to pursue a creative life? What do you give up in order to do that? What do you take up? And with whom are you in solidarity? That has become really complicated in terms of the privileging of certain forms of labour, which is obviously gendered, racialised, able-normative, classed, and evident through disparities in earnings, and in the professionalisation of the cultural sector generally.

That same professionalisation has also resulted in the rise of consultants. This is a problem as the strength of that profession reduces the incentive to create sustainable institutions. In order for consultants, who earn a lot of money per day, to survive, institutions have to not survive. Institutions have to fail.

These are the issues with the sector that London-based writer and artist Morgan Quaintance talks about in his article "New Conservativism: Complicity and the UK Art World's Performance of Progression".[1] We can't take the existence of a cultural sphere run by cultural organisers for granted anymore. That we all work within the cultural sphere doesn't mean anything politically. And it's really hard to accept complicity, or maybe naivety, and the lack of self-criticality of those working in the cultural sector as, for a long time, there's been an unspoken assumption that in the cultural sphere we all have the same values because we like the same artists, books, music. A point that illustrates this well is when architect and scholar Eyal Weizman wrote that the work of poststructuralist philosophers Gilles Deleuze and Felix Guattari was being used by the Israeli Defense Force, everyone was in a bit of a shock – 'Oh my God, this is terrible. We thought that only left-wing liberals could read Deleuze.'

Another way to demonstrate our inability to notice processes taking place outside our milieu that connect directly with these questions of infrastructure is in education: the way we have sleepwalked into the situation where our community of educators is not able to stop the degradation of art education, from a very tangible perspective of disinvestment in art studios and technical cultures, which restricts or informs what type of artist one can become – one that fits the neoliberal mould.

SH   So how would you define cultural infrastructure in relation to your work, for example, with LADA, tdwm studio, or as a co-organiser of the With For About *slow conference* in 2020?

CW   Cultural infrastructure is the support system that enables organisation. Urbanist and academic Abdou Maliq Simone talks about people as infrastructure, and, in this way, those support systems are actually people, which especially came to light in the wake of a pandemic, and in the recognition of systemic, structural racism.

1   Quaintance, M. (2017) 'New Conservativism: Complicity and the UK Art World's Performance of Progression', *e-flux conversations* [https://conversations.e-flux.com/t/the-new-conservatism-complicity-and-the-uk-art-worlds-performance-of-progression/7200]

People being able to call each other up and say, this or that is happening, is a support structure. Within institutions, there should be spaces that are safe for people to discuss problems and to reflect on the structure itself. This support – this infrastructure – should be a system with sufficient resources, or a way in which people can find the tools to do that process of reflection.

SH   What are those support systems made of? Infrastructural support, literally, is synonymous with the enabling of something, and that's done through use. In some ways, it's easy to think about it in terms of an operating system, like a computer, with both functioning hardware and software.

CW   I always find it really difficult to apply these computational systems to human rules.

SH   When I look at institutions, or museum infrastructure, for example, it has become helpful to think about them in their operational terms, or akin to something like roads or doorways, in order to then speak about a more abstract idea of the when and how of an infrastructure's function: where that happens, and what supports it, or what are its conditions, such as policies or theoretical terms.

Producing or enabling systems of care or support can become even more abstract, particularly when you think about the practice of curating. What springs to mind, as an attempt to challenge and work away from these often expandable and co-opted terms, is the think tank *Policy Show*, during 2017 at Eastside Projects in Birmingham, and the work of curators and organisers such as Teresa Cisneros and Lucy Lopez: curators and artists were brought together to conceive of new policies and to draft a set of tangible actions out of these policies. Naming policy within art spaces feels radical: what are the effects of that? What does that do?

CW   A very experienced cultural organiser told me a couple of years ago that you have to make a choice: 'Are you going to dedicate your life to artistic programming, or are you going to dedicate your life to the operational side of things?' And my response was, 'What are you talking about? This isn't a thing. This isn't a choice I need to make.'

But when we think about cultural infrastructure, or organising artistic practice, then what this person was implying is one of the biggest distinctions. There are two different fields, and it's very difficult to walk in both of them at the same time. There are a lot of assumptions about the (im)possibility of operating within both: how they're mutually exclusive, or how the labour that goes into one means that it can't go into the other. And I find this problematic.

SH   The assumptions or the impossibility of doing both?

CW   It's not the assumptions that are problematic, but that there seems to be a situation where both practices can't coexist. It seems that there's something deeply wrong with our modes of cultural organising if it means that the two cannot coexist. The lack of mobility between these two paths is another failure to recognise labour. It's the attitude: 'If we all become middle class, then who's going to clean up? Who's going to clean the toilets?'

SH   Yes, according to Eva Rowson, who is going to do the washing-up? This also wedges a distinction between practice and reflection. A support system should be able to create spaces where the two can coexist: creative work and operation; reflection and practice. Often we feel as though they do, but they don't: what is it to put the thinking to work? This brings to mind the statement you co-wrote with Jade Montserrat, Michelle Williams Gamaker and Tae Ateh, published by *Arts Professional* in 2020, discussing the terms and proclamations of care and solidarity for Black, Indigenous and People of Colour from cultural institutions, which might end up meaningless in the face of both a global public health crisis and continued cases of insidious, structural racism within many institutions of the cultural sector.

CW   Actually, that's a question of scale, because it's about an ability to identify at what scale an action or a proclamation exists. For example, when we consider why Black people and People of Colour are angry at institutions, it's because there are no apologies. Have there ever been apologies? Has the institution ever admitted that it's done anything wrong? And does it understand what it is that it needs to address?
    Those seem like very simple, small and human things. In her work, writer, organiser and educator Mia Mingus reveals how complex and careful these actions, such as apologies, really are. If we think about a scale of publicness, then those are the things that are often at the smallest end of the scale: making them bigger and public would be performing a different type of instrumentalisation. But actually, those private things are maybe the most important, and capitalising on them is at odds with truly engaging with them.

SH   This brings to mind the question of the scale of organisations and institutions, and an individual within these structures. The individual can be at odds with the collective voice of a larger framework (a movement, union, organisation). I'm thinking here specifically about acknowledging the individual's complicity in a larger framework, and the relative ease of speaking as part of a collective voice. This can be a complex situation: an individual can make a statement and gesture wholeheartedly, but an institution has to do that in a much smaller and defined way for it to actually make any structural or systemic shift. So, with a question of scale, is it that the smaller, private gestures are most meaningful?

CW   Possibly so. We see the benefits of that level of care in higher education: the University and College Union (UCU) undertook industrial action in early 2020, demanding that university management address pay, workload, equality and casualisation across educational institutions, and by the middle of 2020, following the murder of George Floyd and the resurgence of the Black Lives Matter movement, we saw due focus on the presence and depth of institutional racism within higher education. For instance, we see this in the Royal College of Art's (RCA) UCU open letter and testimonies of institutional racism, and I've been part of the union organising group co-ordinating this. You can imagine the types of responses we received. As well as a recognition of all the harm that has been done and the need to address it, there have also been individuals questioning whether they have perpetrated racism or contributed to it. Many of them didn't know what to do, and this caused them a lot of stress, but they didn't necessarily pay attention to the problem, which is the harm that has been done to Black, Indigenous and People of Colour.

SH   The difficulty in understanding what harm is, in this context, is striking. Personal and institutional responsibility don't seem to meet: institutions are contested spaces.

CW   Institutions are made up of people, and, in that sense, I really hope that my colleagues at the RCA, and in other organisations, can see that that means *them*. That's supposed to be them, personally. It isn't enough for them to just say, 'Oh,' after the fact, and continue being a silent bystander who apologises afterwards. That's not enough.

What are they doing in order to challenge and make sure that their personal politics, and their understanding of personal politics, add up to institutional politics? You can't just keep on saying that institutional politics look like this or that ... It really irks me that people who are intellectually engaged with these issues feel that they don't have a say in institutional politics. This is a relegation of responsibility. Full stop. They deny responsibility by saying, 'I can't do anything about it.' Of course you can!

And perhaps here I can respond to your ideas about computational systems. When you think about infrastructures as computational systems, then how do the people within this situation that we've just been describing appear? When we talk about infrastructures, we need to recognise the power of individuals within them, or understand that individuals together make a dynamic: they make an atmosphere; they create a situation in which you can, or cannot, talk about things. Or, you can talk about enacting specific principles. This is one of the struggles that I personally have when thinking about computational systems.

SH   I think there are moments where they are helpful. If we talk about infrastructure as a frame within which dynamics, atmospheres, situations occur, it very quickly becomes abstracted from a physical context. And so, to think about those things as part of a system that is based on the unfolding of a scenario, A + B = C, which is then brought to life by people, it clarifies things a little. There's also a question of *who* brings this system to life, as infrastructure is often understood in relation to its *users*.

I think it's important to talk about infrastructure in relation to institutions too, to save it from being an abstracted entity, separate from contested institutions. At least, we have a sense of what institutions are in terms of function/dysfunction.

During the *Talking as Neighbours* programme, we discussed Tate Modern's infrastructure in the context of Tania Bruguera's commission. Across a number of discussions that day, there was an exercise in reading the Tate as a series of infrastructures, rather than just this institution with a symbolic manifestation of art and culture and a material manifestation of two buildings in London, one in Liverpool, and one in St. Ives, a website, a shop, a legacy. In order to read Tate Modern in Southwark, London, specifically, we mapped out everything from the processes and the systems of access that lead a visitor to the door, such as public transport, to the encounters within the building – the vastness of the Turbine Hall and the Tanks – to the idea of feeling comfortable in different spaces, to engagements with the shop, and making a decision about whether to buy a postcard, or the cafe or upon entering into an exhibition. Those conversations were a form of unbuilding dismantling sections or parts of the Tate to understand what it is and see it for what it is.

The Infrequently Asked Questions panel, with Janine Francois, Shaz Hussain, Priya Khanchandani and Tania Bruguera, and the Enacting New Models and Keeping Them Going panel, with Natasha Cox and Eva Rowson, proposed discussions around the responsibilities of people within the institution. And when you think about it in such a fragmented or deconstructed way, suddenly there's not really much that sits at a core, beyond the symbolism of the institution and all the many intersecting elements and figures ... Which is eminently interesting when you want to work infrastructure out!

There's also this idea that people are the core of it because they are the users of an infrastructure that makes it function, which perpetuates the institution, the idea of the institution and its politics. But then, as soon as something breaks, or is challenged, or called on, or questioned, then people disappear, and the institution becomes this very functional system again, where conduits and channels, largely of communication, feel like a black box. What you have then are communication systems, doorways, a series of locked buildings, a series of vistas of the city, and security systems. There are a million different systems: who can be responsible for them, or who can meet that challenge that is made to the institution? Nobody.

CW   Totally. I agree.

SH   There's an impasse that is created between the figuration of an institution and its infrastructure. Going back to your reference to UCU and the university, there are distinct groups of people, with ideas that are defined by their shared values and intentions. And then, there's an impasse between them: neither can take on the other without setting a new precedent for the organisation, or, indeed, neither can cross the threshold into the other without diminishing those values. And those metaphors of operating systems are sometimes helpful to distinguish this complexity on an institutional scale and size, not least, and especially so, when the prospect of arriving at an agreement is concerned.

It's almost as though people flee when something is challenged in institutional infrastructure, and then this system becomes the thing to contend with. I don't mean necessarily the active or transformative type of fleeing in the way that the philosopher Gerald Raunig describes, but these systems left of the institution, in a way, protect people. As soon as there's a challenge, then it's just a series of systems to navigate, like when you need to set up a direct debit for a utility company and you're on hold on the telephone for ages.

So when does it suit someone to be left visible as an individual within the institution, and when does it not suit somebody to become the institution? Sometimes it suits people to be attached to the institution, and other times it doesn't. When it doesn't, there's no one there to speak to, and no one to help you. It just is this working, functioning thing that is sustained through use.

CW   There's also a denial that the institution does harm, that it historically ever did, or could be capable of, or would act in a way that would harm anyone. That's institutional fragility.

SH   And specifically, it involves fleeing from responsibility and accountability.

CW   You mentioned users. The language of users is quite often employed to cover a multitude of different types of positions and interactions. I find that problematic because there's a kernel of inaction, or a lack of responsibility, in a user, in the sense that there is a system that's pre-determined before me, and it will probably exist after me, that I also have limited manipulation of. I don't know what the parameters of manipulation are, or maybe they haven't been made clear to me because someone didn't tell me properly, or I didn't understand fully, or I didn't speak to the right people. There is a limitation to the bandwidth that a user is able to manipulate or is able to work with. And so, instead of being users, I think about how we can be interlocutors with systems.

SH   Institutions will exist before and after us, probably, or they might not. But while we are inhabiting or interacting with them, how can we make sure that they're the best version of the thing that they can be?

CW   That's super important.

SH   What is the relationship between the institution and people? Binding contracts? A lot of this is about the conditions of access to culture, to education, to work. How do we become interlocutors with institutions and infrastructures, rather than users of them? Is there something about solidarity here?

CW   Yes. This refers to what Donna Haraway outlines in *Staying with the Trouble* – where Haraway implores us to learn from the trouble of living *with* a damaged Earth.[2] What might this idea of trouble mean in terms of institutional politics and individual responsibility?

It might mean returning to the question of the separation between the creative work of curating and operations. If you inhabit one or the other of those fields, then you outsource the other function to somebody else. The idea of outsourcing is really important because cultural workers do not usually associate that language with themselves. In other words, holders of creative positions in institutions might not always consider care to be part of their role or responsibility: the wellbeing of an artist, for example, it's the responsibility of human resources, or it might be the informal (and additional) responsibility of somebody who is doing community engagement. There seems to be an inability to engage with those caring aspects of labour. This is a real failure of the way that we, as an industry, have constructed the types of careers that we can have. I think that it's also highly problematic to assume that people who are working within operations are not interested in the creative capacities and the questioning of creative ethics within the institution, especially if you're there to uphold the institution via its infrastructure, like the spokes in a wheel.

SH   Two considerations arise here: one is about communication and the other about value. How can these two sides better interact with one another, and how can labour be equitably revalued, if we are to rethink how infrastructure and institutions, the material and symbolic aspects, work together? What might solidarity look like?

CW   That's really hard to answer. I don't know. This whole thing about the creative work versus the operational side of organisations is part of questioning who is allowed to do artistic labour. What bodies

---

2 Haraway, D. J. (2016) *Staying with the Trouble: Making Kin in the Chthulucene.* Durham, NC, USA: Duke University Press.

are allowed and afforded that privilege? What do those bodies need to forego when they don't do that? So, what does it look like, for example, if a working-class Black woman who was previously working in operations says that they want to be artistic director? What does that mean? And how does that individual come into this situation and feel welcome? And to what extent can they be supported to develop their capacities? It's really important to talk about: many of the conditions that mean that this is even a conversation originate from other fields, so how do we de-hierarchise the work that we do to attend to this?

SH This connects to one of the points that you made at the beginning about the professionalisation of the cultural sphere, manifested in the application of models of business management that are focused on revenue generation, efficiency, and professionalisation at the expense of other things like care and equitable practices.

CW I feel like this has led to an evacuation of responsibility.

SH This is also a mirror of what is happening in education: there's the ouroboros of the snake eating its tail, of the project of education, and then the business model of education. The education project feeds the business model, but the business model doesn't support the education project. There is an evacuation of responsibility within this system. So, there's no one to necessarily refer to when something goes wrong, because the institution has to function as business as usual without concession. Which brings us back to what you said earlier about the often-perceived impossibility of being politically engaged within an institution.

CW Exactly, and shouldn't this quest to address these things be the driver behind solidarity? Or, isn't that what solidarity should look like? There are people who are in the systems that we're discussing, who are being constantly failed by them, and where's the solidarity with them?

In a way, it connects to the question of what is a community? Not a *community of practice*, but a *community-engaged practice*, or a practice that is informed by and made within a community. If the community that is closest to you is the community of artists, and arts workers, and cultural institutions, then the least that you can do is to try and practise with them. For me, when I realised that my community was actually the community that I was called to address, then it meant that I have to do all this unseen work that isn't considered curating in a traditional sense but as operational work.

SH This is the line through our entire conversation. You are speaking about the practise of a life's work. This is the challenge to cultural institutions when we talk about a rethought, reimagined, reconfigured, reorganised infrastructural institution.

CW   It's important to talk about the specificity of what that rethought, reimagined thing is because that is specific to time, it's specific to the individuals who are involved in that project at that time, and the responses, and the legacy of that institution, what has been done, what can be done in the near future. For example, when I was chair of the board at LADA, we went through a period of organisational change. And this relied on an assessment of the capacity of the existing dynamics and a collective capacity for change. Which is interesting because the whole conversation in the cultural sector ten years ago was about assessing our capacity for risk. But it isn't about that anymore, it's about assessing our capacity for change, and given the time we live in, that is inevitable.

SH   Perhaps this is another way to think about cultural infrastructure and institutions: as a shift from risk to change. Though I hesitate, as it still feels gestural; it is still the bravado and clout of a marketised sector.

CW   But then what happens if we put that into a wider societal context and realise that institutions fear the loss of that clout. What happens if we no longer consider them in this way? Then, do we diminish ourselves as a cultural industry, as opposed to the manufacturing realm, or retail realm, or travel?

When considered in this way, that's a bigger problem. We know that there is money; money exists in the world. We are highly critical of that as a sector, especially the ways that we interact with money and commerce, and the ways in which it circulates. There is a lot of discourse about that, but then how do we prevent the sector from disappearing? The inequalities within it are so huge now, so it's very difficult if you're not within an institution to see exactly how you can play a part in changing that dynamic. We continue to grapple with all these factors and thoughts.

Museum Cultures

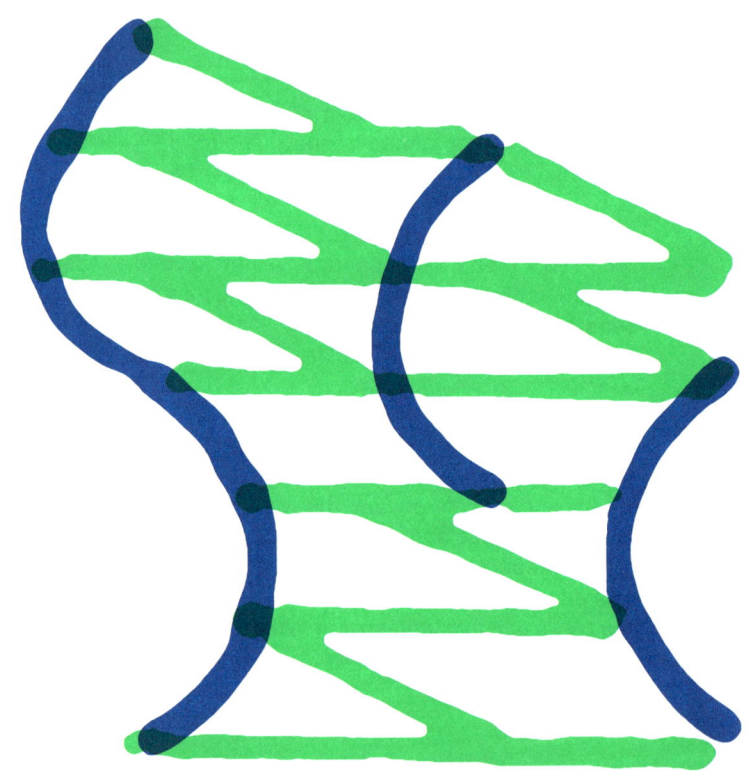

A conversation with Meneesha Kellay [MK]
Wednesday, 4 November 2020. SquadCast, online platform, London

Meneesha Kellay is a London-based curator and cultural programmer across design and architecture. Meneesha has worked across public, private and charitable sector organisations and institutions, and is currently Curator of Design, Architecture and Digital Festivals at the Victoria and Albert Museum (V&A). She is also involved in advocacy for inclusive creative industries. We met to talk online while we were working from our respective homes in South London, during the second wave of the pandemic. I wanted to speak with Meneesha about her work with and within large-scale organisations and institutions to find out what it means to actively work for better inclusion and equitable working practice across the cultural sector, and how 'the museum' might and should reorient itself after 2020 as a culturally sensitive and reflexive infrastructure in a post-digital, post-Brexit, and post-pandemic frame.

○ Accessibility
○ Collaboration
○ Communities

○ Ownership
○ Permission
○ Publics

MK   I equate working within a museum to being a public servant. The museum is a publicly funded civic space, which is intended to represent everyone who feeds into the funding of that space, i.e. the taxpayer. There is often a disjuncture between how museums are read and understood, and how they're performed, to use the language of Theatrum Mundi. Also, within a museum, there are disjunctures in such understanding owing to the hierarchies that make up a museum. This is a really current debate, especially with everything that has happened in 2020. The definition of what a museum is, and who it is for, has also been under debate in recent years.

It's not a static space that simply holds objects, as a space for research, but an active space that is all about creating critical dialogues about pasts and futures: how our pasts inform our futures. There is also a disjuncture between the diverse communities that make up a city like London, where the V&A is located, and the incredible global collection that the museum holds. While it has objects from all over the world, it struggles to reconnect these objects with the communities that have meaning and symbolism within these objects. For example, incredible textiles and ceramics from Nigeria, or the vast Moghul Empire collection that has resonance with South Asian communities in the UK. The museum has thousands of objects from across Africa, but it does not have a permanent Africa Gallery to display these objects. However, work is being done to address this.

There is something that, perhaps naively, I've always thought of as strange about the British Museum: it's got very few British objects in it. You walk around the British Museum, and you see incredible works of art from around the world. Why is it that the British Museum should want to be represented by the Rosetta Stone from Egypt or megalithic statues from Polynesia? I'm not saying that's a bad thing; we just need a deeper reflection upon the fact that we care so much, as a nation, about objects like the Benin Bronzes – which were looted by British soldiers in a raid on Benin City in 1897 – to the point that we don't want to return them to Nigeria. In the same breath, we are living in an age of nationalism where one person can tell another to 'go back to where you came from'. This dichotomy always reminds me of the famous quotation from Ambalavaner Sivanandan, 'We are here because you were there.'

SH   That's such an important introduction to our conversation. How does the term or practice of cultural infrastructure feed into what you do?

MK   I studied architecture, but I didn't necessarily want to be a practising architect. I was interested in everything around and inside the building; everything that influences it; what the built environment contributes, or doesn't to society; and the conversations that it has with the spaces around it.

I've been in the architecture and design worlds for the last fifteen years: I worked at the Architectural Association on its public programme, the Royal Institute of British Architects, and Open City. I ran the Open House programme for a year, which is an incredibly democratic organisation as a charity that opens up buildings to the public across London. Around 250,000 people engage with that festival, usually. I'm now at the V&A, where I curate festivals dealing with design, architecture and digital projects.

I've worked in the public, private, and charity sectors, and now I'm part of a public museum. I have this sense of being a public servant and a duty to represent diverse publics that aren't necessarily represented within the museum's body, or represented enough within that body. That's been a concern of mine to ensure that the work that I do is as thoughtful as possible. It's an ongoing process: it's constantly changing and developing. I collaborate with other groups and other organisations outside the V&A, and that's exciting because it's full of opportunity.

I think cultural infrastructure is such an interesting term, especially in the context of 2020, when the museum was closed intermittently during lockdown. We have previously talked about what a museum means once its doors are closed, as museums have relied on their physical infrastructure for so long, but what happens when it is removed? What does a space like the V&A mean to communities when you can't be within it, or experience the objects directly?

This also puts into question the provenance and the repatriation of objects, because there is an ongoing debate about collections that we hold at the museum: where they're from; who has the ownership or right to those objects. And this leads me to think that if certain objects are so symbolically important to countries and societies around the world, and very few people can actually interact with them directly in a space like the V&A, then perhaps they could be given back, and we could hold copies instead.

The Cast Courts are really impressive spaces within the V&A, full of copies and casts of original works of art and sculpture. They are effective spaces for communicating and translating ideas. So, why can't the museum present other objects in this way and return symbolically important artefacts to the communities where they belong?

I think in 2020 the idea of new cultural infrastructure throws open so many possibilities, a whole realm of interesting debates and questions that museums have actually been grappling with for much longer.

SH   We can talk about cultural infrastructure as being suspended between the material and symbolic resources of an institution as writer and critic Marina Vishmidt defines it. Once the material resource of the museum is inaccessible, then we're left with the symbolic. What is the symbolic in the museum?

MK   It essentially goes back to the roots of the museum. It was originally called the Museum of Manufacturing. It was conceived of as a space in 1851, when the museum was created after the Great Exhibition in Hyde Park, London. It was about educating people as well as exhibiting art. For example, there were displays about food: wax carvings of what a healthy piece of meat looks like and what a rotten piece of meat looks like. It had this real educational, public health aspect to it, which in some ways has been lost because the museum displays – especially the permanent ones – are so finely crafted. I think that element of education as lifelong education for everyone that visited the museum, not just children or young people, is not so present now.

Sometimes I get this feeling when in the museum that everything feels part of a landscape rather than being discrete, individual objects. You walk into the Sculpture Court, for example, or the Silver Galleries, and there's this landscape of beautiful things, and you lose the interesting aspects of one particular object. But maybe I've just been in the museum for too long!

SH   That's a really beautiful and embodied way to describe it. With that idea of the total museum landscape, what does this mean for other institutions, in terms of the art and work in 2020?

MK   I've observed this with visitors to the museum also. Sometimes people walk around the galleries and are looking at objects as though they are part of the building rather than separate objects in and of themselves. So, I keep thinking about its cultural infrastructure, and the museum as this institution: this building in South Kensington, and what it means to close its doors. It's an interesting challenge for museum professionals and curators to be grappling with. How do we make museums relevant to communities beyond the locality of South Kensington, when you can't interact with the museum building and this landscape directly? How do you animate a suburban high street, which during 2020 became busier than spaces like Oxford Street because people couldn't get into central London to do any shopping or sightseeing? Most of us live in a doughnut, in the periphery, and so what role does a museum in central London have to play in that type of space? At the museum, we have our digital space, an entirely different realm where there are also layers of curated objects. When you've got a whole collection to work with, how do you digitise objects to then make them interesting and relevant to people? Is there a new opportunity for, say, Ashanti Gold, that's actually in the museum in a display case? Can we see that in-situ and in context in Ghana through digital technologies and AR and VR? I think there's a whole realm of opportunities, but it's complex.

SH   These shifts preceded the pandemic: the question of repatriating objects; the question of the relevance of collections and exhibitions; and the role of digital interventions. We have a physical manifestation of the museum, and a new question of how it might become mobile, how it might exist beyond its physical space in an urban context. And equally, a shift in the use of digital technologies means that objects are no longer simply found digitally for reference, but instead for a direct experience with them. And we don't have to be at a particular place at a particular time to encounter those objects. The pandemic, in tangible ways, has accelerated some of these changes.

The pandemic has shifted the way we understand, use and value physical places. With universities, as with museums, there's a shift to digital spaces and experiences. But we're left with these vast interior spaces, or landscapes, and we have to rethink the function of cultural and academic institutions accordingly. Perhaps we could talk about this aspect a bit more. What is left of an institution if we can no longer access its buildings? These institutions – museums, universities – are upheld by people, and this links us back to a conversation around responsibility.

MK This is something that we've been grappling with, especially while working from home, which has been such a strange thing for museums. There was a point when forty per cent of the V&A was on furlough during spring and summer of 2020, and then in November everyone went back into the building before the second lockdown. Because being on furlough wasn't just time off, we ended up wondering what our relevance and place in the museum was. After the murder of George Floyd and during the Black Lives Matter protests, we banded together as colleagues to think about what the V&A was going to say in response. The museum put out a statement, which was reinforced by the desire of the staff within the museum to make a statement and show solidarity to the Black community who are part of the V&A community. We self-organised by creating a Museum as a Site of Social (MASS) Action group, which is really interesting because it's an informal network of museums across the world. And we did that not only in response to Black Lives Matter – what the museum can do in terms of anti-racism statements and actions – but also to show solidarity and support for People of Colour within the museum, people who work there.

At the V&A, the MASS Action group was set up, then an Asian Minority Network group and a Disability Network. These self-organised support networks were established really quickly during the furlough, when we didn't have access to each other's private email addresses, but we scrambled to find each other in different ways. For me, that was such an interesting and powerful way for a museum community to express itself.

These methods of care for one another, as an actual community, connects to what I said at the beginning of our conversation about the museum being a community that is publicly responsible and that serves the public, and to do that, we also need to serve each other because we're all aiming towards the same goals. During the furlough, I felt that I'd really joined the museum. So that's one way that this year has enabled forming a working community in a way that isn't necessarily visible to a visitor to the museum, but it strengthens what a museum is and who it's for and how it functions.

SH   In my previous conversation with Cecilia Wee, we talked about different types of solidarity with/in institutions. After all, institutions are people. It is striking how responsibility is configured differently when an institution is not seen as an abstract idea but as people. Hearing you describe how you and your colleagues quickly self-organised while the physical institution was closed, that is, in a sense, absent, is very interesting. It throws into relief the relationship between the individual and the cause of the institution, acknowledging that by being employed by the institution, the individual takes on a specific set of responsibilities, or accountabilities. In a sense, an individual takes on the institution. It seems obvious, but it's often quite a difficult thing to accept. You work at the V&A, and I work at the Royal College of Art, and we take on those institutions, the symbolic and the material parts, and I think it's very easy to forget that totality is implied in our work.

MK   I see what you mean. You play many different roles; you're employed by the institution, but you're also an agitator within it because you're working to make it better and fairer. There's a certain performativity because you represent the museum, and there are things that you can and cannot discuss or do. You're also a member of the public that loves that space. It's a strange duality that you don't necessarily have with a private company, or other organisations, because there are different structures at play, there's not the same type of imaginary. There're a lot of people involved who really love places like the V&A, the British Museum, the Tate, and universities as well, that you feel that you're not only part of them through being a museum professional, or cultural professional, but also because you know that they occupy this public and symbolic space, which contributes to their social and cultural infrastructure. It's another layer to it that isn't quantitative, it's more a feeling which holds a lot of responsibility.

SH   This is an important consideration, particularly when you talk about the creation of the MASS Action group. This taking on the responsibility to self-organise is very similar to a union model: a space that allows for the practice of belief in, and disbelief in, the power of your relationship with the institution.

MK   You're actively working within it to improve it. If you were passive, you wouldn't be part of a union or an activist group. There's a question of love and care here. I think that distinction is important, but also difficult to communicate to upper levels of management within any organisation. Responsibilities are shaped differently. And I think those hierarchies are quite difficult to manage sometimes.

The pandemic has redefined what it means to work. During furlough, our participation in the self-organised group was under question: does this type of work constitute work? We had a philosophical debate about it: is it care for colleagues or care for the institution? Is that work, or is that something that you do out of choice?

I'm part of the MASS Action group. I'm part of the Black, Asian and Minority Network, which we redefined as a Global Narratives Network, and I'm also on the V&A's anti-racism task force that has come about after the Black Lives Matter protests, which is a huge honour and responsibility, and I don't take it lightly. It is so complex to ensure that we, as individuals, come together within that task force to make things happen and to do that quickly enough to feel change, and with the knowledge of what is the most effective change rather than perpetuating the nineteenth-century repository model of a museum. The change needs to be about representing diverse communities, social justice, global equality, planetary wellbeing, reckoning with our colonial past. I'm very cautiously walking into it, consulting as much as possible to ensure that we're doing this process properly.

SH   Can you expand on the idea of doing things properly?

MK   It's about people within the museum: employees who are of colour and how they feel cared for and respected. And there are instances, as there are in organisations around the world, of racism within the institution. Questioning how those are properly dealt with, how we put in place equality, diversity and inclusion training, and how we hold people accountable. There is a focus on the idea that the museum needs to do as much as possible as an organisation to care for its people. And there's the museum as a space for political action and for representing diverse publics.

We need to also look at our object descriptions and our interpretations of history to reinterpret how objects were brought into the museum. Is it stated enough to our audience that certain objects were gained through looting or through wars that were unjust, or through the pillaging of societies? How honest are we with our public and our audience about that?

It's also about who we're attracting to the museum. Are our programmes and exhibitions diverse enough to attract all communities? We're publicly funded, so everyone belongs in these spaces, but we know there are certain groups who never come to the V&A because they don't feel like it's a space for them. They're not represented within it. So what can we do to ensure that they are? There are short and long-term actions, but they can all be done in parallel.

SH   These are the same conversations taking place in universities. It's taken a global pandemic and a very visible and necessary acknowledgement of the work of the Black Lives Matter movement, in the wake of the murder of George Floyd, for institutions to start addressing systemic racism, sexism, trans- and homophobia, classism, and exclusionary practice across every facet of society. It's taken those two moments, which are intertwined, for institutions to even begin, properly, to have these conversations.

> MK   We've reached a breaking point: Black Lives Matter protests; anniversaries of Grenfell and Windrush; disproportionate COVID-19 deaths. They've coalesced into this moment, and we've come to a point where we can't ignore our history, we can't erase it. The removal of the Colston statue in Bristol was a huge event impacting museum culture and prompting questions about how we deal with our histories.

SH   Shifting to an urban perspective, I would like to ask you then, what are the civic and social responsibilities of museums?

> MK   I'll first mention Open House London, which isn't a museum but an organisation that opens buildings to the public that normally can't be accessed. So this line between public and private is very clear, and I think that's how we navigate and read civic spaces: between what we can access and what we can't. And this has been underlined by the pandemic: through restrictions that the government imposed onto our bodies and spaces, including museums. Pre-2020, we were working on a nineteenth-century model of a museum, as a space where there is a clear definition between the objects that are, effectively, private, because you can't touch them, you can just view them from a distance, and the public spaces which you do have access to. This static relationship with the museum, an arm's-length analysis of its spaces, which you don't necessarily feel ownership of, is now coming under question.
>
> The role of the museum is to reanalyse global issues, to look at society, wellbeing, and our responsibility to one another. I don't think these have been priorities for museums in the past. I see the shift and change in the museum's relationship to the city and how we understand civic spaces: what we have access to and what we don't. It's a tricky one because it evolves as our relationship to space changes, especially in the light of the pandemic, which made us more community-focused, operating often within a radius of metres rather than miles – hyperlocal. Going into the city centre is something that we don't necessarily need to do anymore. There's now a question of why you would do that, what kind of experience you would want to have, and what engagement with spaces you'd like to have. Cultural infrastructure extends beyond what we know as the traditional heart

of a city into this idea of a polycentric city, and a polyphonic experience of a museum.

SH   What does that mean infrastructurally? Do polycentric cities and polyphonic museums require new models?

MK   New models are a really key aspect. It's also about looking at what the museum does and how it functions, about it being more collaborative and looking at new typologies. How can we make museums more accessible as spaces for education? Can we learn from the museum if we can't access it? If a library is full of books, and a museum is full of objects, what can we learn from those objects if we can't take them out? In commissioning terms, how do we speak to other disciplines: choreographers, sound artists, visual artists, designers? How do we tap into their knowledge and resources and open up the museum to them and say, how can we share this knowledge further in ways that we, as the museum, can't necessarily do through an experience solely within the museum? How can the objects we have in the museum collection be interpreted by and through artists and other means? The idea of a collective voice makes me think of the multiple interpretations of an object, and this is a key challenge for interpretation departments in museums at the moment. We're not all looking at the same object and interpreting it in the same way, because we come to a space with a whole host of influences and approaches to reading. So, how do we take one object and give it multiple voices and meanings?

SH   That feels strangely radical! We return to the question of what it takes for museums – as gatekeepers of historical narratives that articulate colonial violence, abuses of power, the very idea of authorship, etc. – to step up through radically changed practice in interpretation departments and enable those multiple voices you describe.

MK   Museums uphold this really dated idea that they are purveyors of knowledge. In fact, it is often the curator that holds the keys to a certain reading of a certain time period, collection or set of objects. What the curator is doing through their practice supports – or not – the idea of a museum that's outdated.

SH   The curator is an interesting figure to use as an example of what's at stake here, what the problems are, what could be better. The practice of curating sits at a point that interfaces with different components of the museum: hierarchies of labour, audiences, contributions to disciplinary narratives, technical or operational negotiations, and relationships that people have with the space of the institution. The curator, in this way, moves across the institution. New infrastructural approaches might involve using some of those access points (to labour and care, audiences and narratives, technology, logistics and space) to rethink some of the relationships within the museum.

MK Curatorial practice is also no longer museum specific. It comes back to relinquishing control. I don't want to discount what curators do at all because I think it's so important to have a really thorough understanding of a subject area. In the context of the challenges of welcoming all possible audiences to a museum, the only way to open that up is to allow for different types of interpretation. Otherwise, we're just speaking the same language over and over again. I think it's really important for people to realise that we're all fallible: history is too. Also, we don't necessarily know everything within the museum, and it's important to look at collaborations as a way of expanding our knowledge.

SH Interpretation departments are sites for this to happen within museums. Is crowd-sourcing interpretation possible? Should wall texts, for example, be temporary and mutable?

MK Yes, that's a conversation that we're having at the V&A. We have millions of objects in the collection, and we are currently trawling through them and finding descriptions written thirty years ago. Those descriptions may be incorrect, and so interpretation by committee, allowing for multiples, might be an idea.

Or, we get into the territory where the interpretation of an object may be factually correct but misses its imaginary, affective and emotive appeal, or the possibilities of what that object can be in different contexts. I think this is a really interesting site for discussion when it comes to exhibitions. There's a whole history behind each acquisition, and why something is supposedly important, how that's interpreted, why, and to whom. This is something that museums are constantly grappling with. It's not a straightforward question, which is why there are so many objects that are open to multiple viewpoints. I think this will continue to be a major challenge for museums in years to come. It's not something that we'll solve anytime soon, I'm sure.

SH Outside of the museum, maybe we can now talk about other conditions that might make cultural infrastructure. I'm thinking here of accidental or incidental institutions or infrastructure.

MK It links to the idea of cultural institutions going into communities, and how this process can be relevant, and representative of diverse communities and cultures, which is a huge challenge for museums. Museums are grappling with how to bring communities and cultures into a museum setting in a meaningful way that isn't tokenistic. Are we only representing what's popular to a certain part of society?

The idea of accidental institutions is a really tricky one because it's almost like labelling a cultural output in a way that doesn't need to be labelled. Do you see what I mean? It's so difficult to think about this because we have recently been so detached from the spaces that are so energising, like a music venue or club, or spaces for dancing, or for expressing ourselves in other ways. These examples are such a huge part of our cultural infrastructure because they provide meaningful connections with people; encountering strangers in an enclosed space is physically enriching. There are so many qualities that constitute and make up that space. I think any replication of that in a museum setting would feel false. I think museums do struggle with accurately, and properly, harnessing popular culture within their collections and within their spaces in a way that doesn't feel contrived and staged.

Those spaces and those experiences define cities. They're all, and I hate this phrase, kind of high and low culture. There has to be a better way of describing them because you can be as enriched from dancing in a sweaty club as spending a day in a museum. It's so intertwined with what it means to be in a city and how well, or not, a city functions. Especially a place like London. No one comes here for the weather; they come for the culture. And that's in all respects: from museums to skateparks, to clubs, and everything in between.

To create the infrastructure to allow for those things to happen is a built-environment professional's responsibility. You can't gentrify a space through crass and arbitrary delineations of space for some things to happen within; this needs to be done more subtly, allowing for something to happen rather than restricting it. For example, if an architect sketches out an arbitrary space for a skatepark, people probably wouldn't use it, because it's not designed by skaters. It's that sort of bandwidth or that subtlety that's important.

A New Cultural Institution

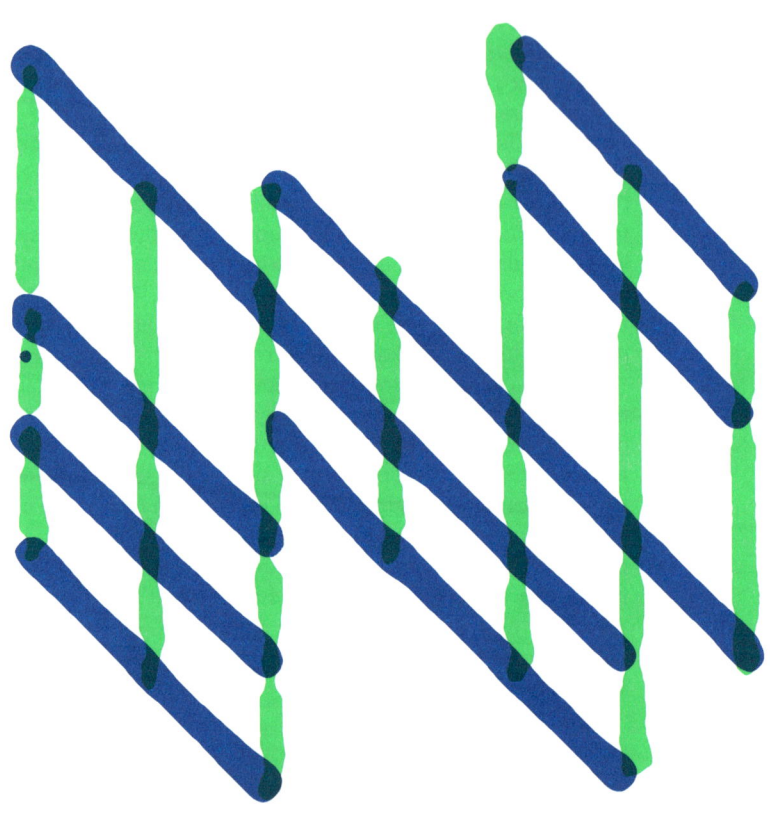

A conversation with Marta Michalowska [MM] and John Bingham-Hall [JBH]
Monday, 7 December 2020. SquadCast, online platform, London

Marta Michalowska and John Bingham-Hall are co-directors of Theatrum Mundi and are based in London and Paris, respectively. Marta is also a writer and director of The Wapping Project in London. John is also a cities researcher and organiser. Together they work closely with a small team of researchers and architects at Theatrum Mundi, a centre for research and experimentation in the public culture of cities. We met to talk online at the beginning of the third lockdown in London. I wanted to speak with Marta and John about their work as co-directors of Theatrum Mundi as they navigate the scale and range of research projects, programmes and collaborators that the organisation is engaged with; the process of transition from a research project and network attached to the London School of Economics (LSE), to becoming a charitable incorporated organisation and research centre; and the challenges the organisation faces in putting research to work ethically, equitably and responsibly.

○ Hosting
○ Modularity
○ Production

○ Reflexivity
○ Scale
○ Solidarities

SH　　As a starting point, what do you do, and what is cultural infrastructure in relation to that?

MM　　I work across two organisations – Theatrum Mundi and The Wapping Project – and there are certain similarities between them. They both have been created to produce work – research and creative work, respectively – rather than be places where you go to experience culture. That said, one of them, The Wapping Project, had almost become its own infrastructure – the building where it was based – and, since it sold that space, it's been trying to answer the question of how you can separate the institution, the portable core of the organisation, from the place that is associated with the institution. Together with my co-director there, we answered this question of what lies at the core by saying that the aim of The Wapping Project is to support artists and make new work. The organisation is about creating opportunities for people to do things that perhaps wouldn't happen in other circumstances. And I think that's what created the institution. The infrastructure of this institution is the will to create space for making new work. I also bring this ethos to my work at Theatrum Mundi. I think that at the core of Theatrum Mundi is the desire to create space for open conversation, which in itself can be an infrastructure, because there is so little space for open-ended conversation within cultural institutions. This is perhaps due to funding structures that focus on easily definable outcomes. Both Theatrum Mundi and The Wapping Project are more open-ended organisations in their ways of working.

JBH　　I'd never thought about that parallel. Also, Theatrum Mundi used to be part of the LSE, which is very much a physical space in central London. And some of our current publication formats or practices are inheritances from academic ways of working. I think recently it's become clear to me that some of our less useful or sustainable practices are likely inheritances from that academic space. It sounds so obvious, but we now pay people for everything, as much as possible, which was not the case in the academic model.

　　Recently, we had an event – the third in a series of annual colloquiums – which was based on a call for papers, and it felt very different to our other programmes. In a university setting, people often pay to use the platform that you create for them to communicate their research – like a conference, for example. That seems so out of kilter with the way we work now. That particular format is also one where you put a call out and just see what comes back to you, and, even though it's open, you're much less able to consciously reshape existing barriers, or biases, as to who's going to respond. The open call is structured by barriers and inequalities.

　　We've also increasingly shifted away from straight panel discussion or talk formats to combine different forms of communication through live performance, film, etc. That would have been very difficult to do in the lecture theatre at the LSE. We never did a performance there. With hindsight, I don't know why not. It's taken a bit of time to gain the confidence to commission and programme performance as a format for sharing research. This is, in part, owed to Marta, whose background and experience supports different forms of production and communication from talks, to readings, to performance.

So, Theatrum Mundi's infrastructure, or underlying patterns, or even ideas of how things work, certainly comes from being part of a bigger institution, and other external influences. In November 2017, we left the LSE and began operating as an independent charity. I think it's taken at least three quarters of that time since November 2017 to get to a point of establishing our identity, especially in terms of balancing our ways of working. I think our identity, in terms of research, was already present and quite clear, even if we now have richer means of exploring that, but we needed to refine and develop an institutional practice and define how value is produced at different levels of the organisation. Specifically, how that value is reinvested, into what, and what comes from that value as different scales of thinking and making.

MM   Susannah, you brought these questions and considerations into Theatrum Mundi through your fellowship. We probably wouldn't be having this conversation otherwise. The programme you co-curated at Tate Exchange, *Talking as Neighbours: Re-Imagining the Institution*, and your broader research, created a platform for reflecting what institutions are, and where Theatrum Mundi sits within the cultural landscape. I don't think we had been consciously thinking about these questions before. Perhaps they would have come out in some way, but they certainly hadn't been so clearly present before you joined us as a fellow. In a way, Theatrum Mundi is an institution in the making. It's a very young organisation, as an independent charitable organisation, even though it has a much longer history. We seem to be reflecting on institution-making while we're in the middle of doing it. This is probably a very rare occurrence.

JBH   I think one of the tensions for us about this reframing of the organisation as an institution is the proximity between doing and reflecting. What do we mean by the word institution? Everyone within the organisation is a maker of some kind: doing writing, doing research, doing sound editing, making creative work. But we're also hosts, and hosting is a really complicated practice to get right. We've learned that the hard way through mistakes in hosting in other institutional contexts. It is difficult to do both: make the work and be the host; be the voice and the platform.

So, does the institution always need to be only the host? If you have an institution where the members of it are also its voices and performers, could that lead to solidarities between artists and institutional workers? What happens when there's not a clear division between those positions? Would an artist we invite into the organisation then work together as a peer with the organisation?

SH   I love the idea that becoming an institution might be resolved through thinking about what hosting means. Hosting in a careful and caring sense is when we think about people: the who of the institution, the identities, the bodies of the institution, and the necessary systems of care around them. Hosting is also about being propped up by supporting structures, which is often what we talk about in relation to infrastructure. So, it's at once a form of kinship and intimacy, and the manifestation of four walls, or a space, that is defined by its material institutional qualities.

JBH   I think one of the problems with big institutions is that the people working within them are not valorised as their creative selves as much as they should be. And so, maybe those solidarities can come from institutions acknowledging that they are a set of voices already, before they look at which voices they even invite in.

I get the sense that in spaces and galleries, or institutions, that are closer to our scale, there are people whose role is to sustain the infrastructure, and who are never authors. Those people are never given an opportunity for authorship within the organisations that employ them. At Theatrum Mundi, the exact opposite is true, but this does create tensions. Moving in and out of being an author, and getting individual credit for work, and then doing work that disappears into the larger organisational structure is difficult. I think there is a potential for solidarity within organisations – or understanding of these different positions – by allowing employees to occupy both roles: authorship and collective infrastructural maintenance.

MM   I think in large institutions, the person who has the voice is often the curator for a major exhibition, for example. In most cases, they do not do this on their own – there's a large team working with them – but it's that lead curator that is put on a pedestal. I have a bit of a problem with current curatorial practices drawing too much attention to themselves, where curating as a word means to care. And, for me, the role of a curator is to make the work of artists shine and not to shine the light on themselves. I feel that the curatorial role should be more similar to the role of a producer in other mediums. Perhaps a humbler practice. But that's an aside. What I find interesting is the question of whether a dance or theatre company is an institution? Perhaps Theatrum Mundi resembles these kinds of organisations more than an art institution. We are certainly not like the Tate, or even smaller cultural organisations that are venue-based.

JBH   Do you not see what we're doing as curation in a way?

MM   I think what we do at Theatrum Mundi is more production than curation. We create possibilities for new work to emerge, while maintaining a strong intellectual practice of thinking about the processes required for the making of the work. There's a collective mode of practice within production-orientated organisations, where everyone involved brings in their expertise to create a production, whether for stage or elsewhere. The production cannot exist without each individual element, it can only exist when all the elements come together. The name Theatrum Mundi makes quite a lot of sense to me: we are bringing a lot of individuals that come from very different worlds to create something bigger. And it is through synergy that each of the voices within the organisation create something a lot more ground-breaking than each could create in isolation. This can only happen through the interlocking of different practices.

I'm producing podcasts at The Wapping Project. These are conversations with artists with whom the organisation worked throughout its history. What comes across strongly in those conversations is the issue of constraints imposed on artists in the majority of art galleries and institutions. Artists are often met with restrictions they have to push against. They are told, 'You can't do this. This is not possible.' Or, 'You can't drill here.' There seems to be a lot of pressure to make work that is convenient: does not create too much mess; is not causing trouble in maintenance; it can be photographed, archived and written about afterwards. While in performance production, transformation of space is a natural process within the making of work.

I talked to the artist Jane Prophet who created an installation for the opening of the Wapping Hydraulic Power Station in 2000. Her work had been primarily in video before. She had an idea, and other curators told her, 'This is not possible. This is never going to happen.' Then she met Jules Wright, the founder of The Wapping Project, and gave her a drawing of her idea. Jules said, 'This is amazing. How do we make this happen?' And the installation became a reality: the main gallery space of the building was lined with black vinyl to create a pool that was then flooded, and above it, 120 electroluminescent cables were suspended, which reflected in the water, creating an infinity effect. This was technically complicated and required solutions that ensured that every element worked over the duration of the exhibition. How do we use what we have, and the expertise we have or can access, to make this project happen, rather than attempt to reduce the idea to something that is easier to handle? Where do you get a company that can flood a building without destroying it? Where do you get an engineer who can make these electroluminescent cables to do what we want them to do? I would say that this is an infrastructural approach.

JBH   Yes, rather than the building shaping the format of the work, the work reshapes the building.

SH   I'm interested in thinking about what that means in terms of an organisation, as, when we talk about a building, an identity, there's a necessary ecology in question. But when we talk about something being production-orientated, parts of that are stripped away. We might find that what is left are the relationships and an ethos generated by people, and the idea that things always just work out. We often hear about things just working out, in hindsight. So whether things work out, out of necessity, or because one manages to find resources, or whether one just makes it happen through drawing on the network of people, there's a default sensibility of things just working out in art.

MM   I think, ultimately, this all boils down to the question of risk, and to what extent an organisation is willing to take it. To make challenging projects happen, an organisation needs to factor in a possibility of failure. In making work that pushes boundaries, whatever the medium, one goes through the constant process of nearly failing, and at times completely failing, and gathering everything one has available, and more, to work out how to solve encountered setbacks.

JBH   The degree to which one can take risk relates to what one has responsibility for and who you have responsibility to. The interesting thing about a building is if it is purpose-built, like the South London Gallery in Camberwell, London, for example. It was built as a platform for art accessible to a geographical community in a part of the city that was underserved by cultural provision. Running that building, one becomes responsible for moderating access to that platform. That's a radically different thing to what we do at Theatrum Mundi. I wonder whether there's something about an institution's responsibility for taking care of a piece of physical infrastructure and deciding how it gets used, by who, for what purpose, and to communicate what?

MM   Risk is intertwined with trust, which is very often where large institutions fail. And trust is linked with responsibility. So, if someone says to you, 'why don't you do it,' and you've never done anything like this before, you will really want to achieve, you will put in an incredible amount of effort, because you won't allow yourself to fail, you will do everything not to let down those who trusted in you. You may struggle, and things might not always work, but you will just make it the best you can. You will take personal responsibility for making it the best you can. And maybe you'll get help from someone. I think the problem with large organisations is that people who are not artists, curators or directors are rarely given space to take responsibility.

JBH   I wonder whether one of the reasons for that goes back to this idea of inheriting infrastructure versus creating infrastructure. In inheriting an institution, or building, even if it was born out of a private initiative, rather than something that was presented by the government, you inherit the cultural platform and take on a responsibility for its history and legacy, and it's not so much a division between public and private. Whereas, if you're creating a new platform, that thing is constantly changing as it emerges; there's something very different about emergence and inheritance with infrastructure and the responsibility that difference brings.

SH   There are different scales and different realities of risk-taking. People are involved, and operation and authorship are invoked; equally, different models (production-orientated versus exhibition-focused) invoke different practices. This becomes interesting when thinking of organisations such as Theatrum Mundi. What are the conditions of risk for Theatrum Mundi, a becoming institution? If we think about risk-taking defined as an ability to respond to people, things, structures, buildings, discourse, this also requires the naming of that risk. What underwrites risk-taking is an acceptance of the precarity and the instability of a practice, a programme, an approach to hosting, or making space for people, which shines a different light on that precarity. We often think about it in relation to labour, but when you think about it in terms of the stability of a set of principles, or of an institution, I think it opens up a different type of question about solidarity.

The cultural sector is very much based on risk, either financial or in terms of labour or sustainability. The culture of the sector is altogether risky. And this is because the sector is often triangulated between market, legacy and participation. This question of risk and its conditions comes at a time, which I think is important to note, after Coco Fusco's call for new commitments practised in and through institutions in her article 'We Need New Institutions, Not New Art',[1] published on 26 October 2020. This call exposes the urgency of transformation needed within the cultural sector, and the necessity to, in the words of Morgan Quaintance 'create avenues for funding separate from exploitative networks, organising spaces or gallery spaces with a sense of civic responsibility, and devising opportunities for new, critical voices that are invisible in such a sector.'[2]

The idea of self-sustaining is another important point to add to the mix; it's what you've both been speaking about, with The Wap-

---

1   Fusco, C. (2020) 'We Need New Institutions, Not New Art', *Hyperallergic* [https://hyperallergic.com/596864/ford-foundation-creative-futures-coco-fusco/]
2   Quaintance, M. (2017) 'New Conservativism: Complicity and the UK Art World's Performance of Progression', *e-flux conversations* [https://conversations.e-flux.com/t/the-new-conservatism-complicity-and-the-uk-art-worlds-performance-of-progression/7200]

ping Project, and also connects to what Andrea Phillips called for in new models of solidarity between different types of cultural institutions or practices during the final panel discussion on solidarity at *Talking as Neighbours: Re-Imagining the Institution.*

JBH   When I did my PhD at The Bartlett School of Architecture at University College London, my research unit, Space Syntax, had this very spatial way of understanding societal organisation: there is an institution when a spatial form and an organisational form become coherent. So, in a building, you have departments, and they all have physical spaces. A department operates a specific part of the building, and another department operates another part of the building, and that matrix sustains an institutional structure. Practically, we don't think of Theatrum Mundi in this way. We don't say, 'Here's our publishing department, here's our media department, here's our research platform', where people are editors, or authors, or researchers, or event hosts. Maybe we should. What's interesting is that everyone in the organisation is in all of the departments, and we understand each department as a different way of operating. For example, when we are hosting an event or workshop, we have to remind ourselves of what that entails as a form of practice, in terms of just how you invite people, how you step back, how your job is to set an ethical framework for a conversation.

For Theatrum Mundi, it's very difficult to keep any sense of a structured division. Whether that's a good thing or a bad thing, I don't know. But what makes us not yet an institution is just that. We had an advisory meeting last year where there were two camps: one wanted us to institutionalise, to have a much clearer working structure; the other, with Jayden Ali spearheading, told us that we are a collective practice and that we should try to avoid institutionalising.

We must decide which route to take. I do want to take on a physical space: an open platform for hosting experimentation, a workshop space, where we can host researchers alongside our team. If we had this, though, we might lose that quite productive interpenetration between authoring, hosting, making, operations, public events, etc.

MM   To me, Theatrum Mundi is a young institution. It has the hallmarks of an institution, but not a space-based one. I'm wondering how as organisations grow, they can preserve that very early ability to respond, to rally people around something, to experiment. Is there a way to preserve some of that very fresh, imaginative, and perhaps, at the same time, chaotic way of working that defines the early stages of organisations? This takes me to a question about the relationship between the vision and the institution. A vision can change because it is connected to a point of view. When the situation changes, the vision can be adjusted. But maybe there are elements of an institution that must be stable.

JBH   That reminds me of a practical consideration: if all of us were to leave Theatrum Mundi and hand it to a new group of people, what are we handing on? What outlasts us? There has to be something that defines what an institution is. The institution needs to be responsive to the voices within it, but also, and maybe this is the problematic part of an institution, there must be something lasting, something that can be handed on. Those things are probably the stickiest and most stubborn and most conservative parts of an institution. They must be the deep assumptions that no individual person can come in and dismiss by saying, 'But that's crazy. We can't do it like this.' I don't think we have any of that, but maybe I'm wrong.

SH   You've just highlighted something that I've been thinking about: the idea of institutional legacy. You have also talked about inheritance, which I think is one of the most critical parts of this whole conversation because it speaks to the idea of what you have or have not inherited from the LSE, for instance, but also, and more broadly, this feeds into the ongoing conversation about large institutions stepping up to acknowledge their own problematic historical and cultural inheritances.

One brilliant illustration of this idea of working against institutional legacy is the School of the Damned, which Sean Roy Parker and I discuss in the first conversation in this publication. It's an alternative MFA programme, more recently framed as an arts and education platform, which was set up in 2013 in response to the increasing financialisation of universities. Born out of disenfranchisement with the state and status of art education in the wake of the economic crisis of 2008, the project reforms itself anew, entirely, with each cohort.

Something connected to this is a consideration of scale. When you talk about the modular restructure of Theatrum Mundi, how does scale fit into it? Thinking of large-scale institutions as a point of reference, we are asking what infrastructure is, where it is located: is it people, is it labour, is it movement? And what happens between each of these components? Where does Theatrum Mundi's infrastructure lie? How does this work for an organisation that, on one hand, resembles a collective, and on the other, has to be concerned with revenue streams and paying collaborators (not that these should be separate, but we know they often are). In many ways, the organisation is already working in a modular way.

MM   Part of that problem is the capitalist conditioning that focuses on constant growth, and measuring success through growth. Does Theatrum Mundi have to become bigger? Does an institution have to become bigger? Maybe it's okay to have ten people and no more. I think the idea that if you create something, for example, you open one shop, then you must open another shop, and then another, and then, after a while, you've created an empire. Do you always need to aim for an empire?

> JBH That modular structure is already present, and Marta is right – we have a way of working which has a clear limitation in terms of number of people – and rather than shifting and changing the way of working, I think it's better to consciously limit the number of people that are on the payroll. Not that we're fighting off money that could enable us to grow to become an organisation five times the size, but if we were, I think it would still be worth saying that we have a model that works up to about this size, and we'd rather spend time refining or learning more about how that model works.
>
> Our diagram of Theatrum Mundi illustrates the workings of the organisation: the backstage, the onstage, and the research and development. So, there is a conceptual division. Rather than creating the usual departments that constitute an institution, it presents the ways of working of the organisation. I think it's helpful for people to see how the different things they do fit into a bigger structure. Even with only eight employees, people don't always know what's going on in every part of the organisation.

SH What are your reflections on this current moment: when cultural institutions are called to acknowledge and work to redress systemic violence and institutional fragilities that, in turn, are the preserve of racist and inequitable institutions. What is the opportunity here for cultural organisations and infrastructures to be rethought, reconfigured, and reorganised?

> JBH This is a very difficult question. The Black Lives Matter movement has been very active for several years now, but in this moment of outpouring and awareness and self-interrogation that came after the death of George Floyd, my initial response was to say, 'we need to pay attention to why we aren't more diverse.' And actually, that was a mistake because it didn't take account of the diversity there already was amongst our team. So I think the first opportunity is to open up an internal conversation about the range of experiences coming from the diverse backgrounds already represented in the organisation, and to foreground opportunities for the knowledge coming from that to shape what we are doing. At the same time, there was an urgent need and an opportunity to reshape the higher levels of the organisation, such as the board, and that was something we were able to do, as we are growing, and there is unformed space to grow into.

MM We could spend a lifetime trying to answer this question. I think it should be there as part of an address that recurs all the time.

And being a small organisation doesn't always mean that you are less influential in this respect, or that you should be growing to become bigger and replace the current major institutions.

JBH   What's most difficult for us is to carve out dedicated space for 'action groups' or 'task forces', because all of our core resources are used just to keep the organisation running. I know that all cultural institutions in the UK are facing scarcity of different kinds, and it seems that the bigger ones, at least, have the capacity that could be invested into that reshaping. But in this sense, I think we're lucky that we are emergent, and we can build these politics into our institution-making rather than having to try to insert them remedially. Although we have a lot of assumptions, we don't have the established deep infrastructures that certain institutions do. I think that the opportunity for us is to find ways to invite different people into the organisation, but here is also an issue of capacity: it is difficult because we're just about managing financially to shape things so that everyone who is already with us, stays with us. We're not able to create a new role for someone to come in and work on diversity, which is also a very problematic positioning of someone within an organisation. So, for us, it's about the choices we make when we invite collaborators, contributors, speakers. That's what we can do at this point: pay attention to who we invite, who we pay, and work against the replication of privilege. How do we distribute resources, and to what extent are we responsive to what happens? How does this then change an institution?

MM   In many ways, this connects to the idea of risk, but not only risk at an institutional level. There is a personal element to this through the need to understand other experiences, being genuinely interested in them, trying to see things from different perspectives. It's a risk to engage with a completely different group of people and with completely different views and/or experiences. Rather than doing diversity by percentages – you have this many per cent of people who represent either Black or Queer or other marginalised groups – you can ask yourself: what is the experience of living, being that other person in this context? And I think one needs to become uncomfortable at times. These things require a degree of personal risk-taking that enables a questioning of the structures – broken yet still often invisible infrastructure – that support the perpetuation of racism, sexism, classism, homophobia or xenophobia.

SH   Risk-taking in this way is also taking on the armatures of institutions and putting them to work in new, better ways.

Contributors

Sean Roy Parker is an artist, environmental educator and fermentation enthusiast based at DARP artist community in rural Derbyshire. His work examines the life cycle of materials, complexities of civic responsibility, and problem-solving through collaborative action. He practises traditional approaches to craft and art-making, using leftover or abundant items of nature and artifice to explore feelings of eco-anxiety in late-stage capitalism and redistribute resources through flexible care structures like labour exchanges and favours. He recently produced a learning project for Liverpool Biennial on bacteria titled *A Processing Medium*, 2021, and was in residence at Pols, Valencia, in September 2021, researching anarchist, anti-gentrification solidarity with the peasant farmer network. @fermental_health

Cecilia Wee is a fellow of the Royal Society of Arts, an independent curator, educator and agitator who grew up in London. Her work addresses equitable infrastructures for art and social action, interconnectedness and relationships within and beyond capitalism, working with practitioners using experimental sound, performance, visual and design practices. Cecilia has edited books, curated exhibitions and events, and led research projects with organisations in the UK and Europe. Cecilia wrote her PhD on the documentation of Live Art, and is Visiting Tutor in Visual Communication at the Royal College of Art, and founder of tdwm studio.

Meneesha Kellay is a curator based in London. She currently leads contemporary programming at the Victoria and Albert Museum (V&A), commissioning projects and installations, and curating events and displays for the London Design Festival and London Festival of Architecture, among others. Previously, she was Public Programmes Curator at the Royal Institute of British Architects, ran Open House London 2014, and produced talks and events at the Architectural Association. Meneesha has been on the Royal Institute of British Architects Architects for Change Advisory Board, was appointed to the 2019 London Festival of Architecture Curation Panel, and is a Steering Committee Member for Design Can. She has been appointed to the V&A Anti-Racism Task Force and is passionate about decolonising cultural institutions.

Marta Michalowska is a curator, producer, artist and writer based in London. She has recently completed her novel *Sketching in Ashes,* supported by Arts Council England through the Developing Your Creative Practice programme, and is currently writing her second, *A Tram to the Beach*, both exploring contested territories. Marta is Associate Director of Theatrum Mundi and Director of The Wapping Project. She has been commissioning and producing artists' work, and curating and organising exhibitions and public programmes for well over a decade.

John Bingham-Hall is Director of Theatrum Mundi and an independent researcher based in Paris. With a background in music (Goldsmiths) and architectural theory (Bartlett, University College London), his broad interest in the staging of shared life in cities takes shape through the analysis and making of performance, infrastructure, and media. Since 2015, he has initiated projects on cultural infrastructure, urban commons, and sonic urbanism; collaborated on research projects at the London School of Economics and University Oxford; taught at Central Saint Martins College of Art and Design and University College London; published writing across scholarly and arts platforms; and organised queer cultural events (serving drinks whenever needed). John is the 2021 Banister Fletcher International Fellow at the University of London Institute in Paris.

Susannah Haslam is a researcher and educator based in London. She is a tutor in humanities at the Royal College of Art in London and a research fellow with Theatrum Mundi. She collaborates with Tom Clark via the research group adpe, with whom she has co-produced a reader on unbuilding infrastructure (annotating. institutions.life). Her current research navigates the relationship between contemporary education and cultural institutions and infrastructures; queer and critical subjects, pedagogies, practices and environments; tertiary-level education alternatives and expansions. Susannah wrote her PhD on the Educational Turn in art and alternative art education, and previously studied visual cultures.

Acknowledgements

The texts in this Edition are based on transcripts of four conversations that I had with Cecilia Wee, John Bingham-Hall, Marta Michalowska, Meneesha Kellay, and Sean Roy Parker between 2020 and 2021, as part of my fellowship at Theatrum Mundi, within the Making Cultural Infrastructure (MCI) project. They are framed by my ongoing research into the complex of relationships between cultural institutions and cultural infrastructures, specifically those between educational and art contexts in the UK.

The fellowship began in 2019 with a public programme *Talking as Neighbours: Re-Imagining the Institution* at Tate Exchange, which I co-organised alongside John, Marta and Cecily Chua from Theatrum Mundi, and with Tram Nguyen and Annie Bicknall from Tate Modern. This day of discussions was programmed in response to Tania Bruguera's 2018-19 Hyundai commission *10, 148, 451*. Janine Francois, Priya Khanchandani, Shaz Hussain and Tania Bruguera convened the first discussion framing some of the difficult and complex realities of being women of colour in the cultural sector, allyship, and problematising the notion of artist-as-saviour. Zinzi Minnott configured a space for movement to share ongoing enquiry into the motion and queering of bodies in institutional spaces. Tash Cox and Eva Rowson shared some of their work on horizontal models of cultural organising, starting with questions of access: how do we arrive at a museum; how do we enact practices of care within them, and then keep them going? Yuri Pattison shared ongoing work that subjugates the material and technical infrastructures of culture in urban and online sites. Andrea Phillips, Natalie Bell and Irit Rogoff each presented a critical reflection and position on the relationship between infrastructure and new types of institutions through the lens of solidarity.

The question of how artists can make meaningful impact on a museum's infrastructure marked the first point of research, but following *Talking as Neighbours: Re-Imagining the Institution*, it felt necessary to extend those discussions outside of a specific museum to acknowledge the range of realities of labour conditions, work, and the complexities of the relationships that different actors have within, with, and outside of institutions, not least the geography, staging and functioning of buildings, and the institutional legacies at play about them. At the beginning of 2020, I began to plan for a series of Workroom Conversations at Theatrum Mundi with an aim to extend each of the above discussions by inviting a group of cultural organisers and practitioners working in London. This plan became impossible during the early stages of the COVID-19 pandemic, and so, Sean Roy, Cecilia, Meneesha, Marta and John very generously gave their time, energy and thinking to my project via a series of dialogues, mostly online. Dialogues are structuring metaphors for sustained conversation based on commitment and care: the edited conversations included in this publication were spoken from places of active, critical, considered, and hard work, experience, deftness, and sensibility. Through them, this spidery term 'cultural infrastructure' and the practice of infrastructuring was afforded rich and textured life. Each dialogue opened its own novel discourse on discrete praxes of cultural infrastructure in London, and specifically throughout 2020 and its immediate afterwards.

Thank you to Tram Nguyen, Annie Bicknall, Tania Bruguera, Janine Francois, Priya Khanchandani, Shaz Hussain, Zinzi Minnott, the Tate Neighbours, Tash Cox, Eva Rowson, Yuri Pattison, Andrea Phillips, Natalie Bell and Irit Rogoff for setting things in motion. Thank you to Sean Roy Parker, Cecilia Wee and Meneesha Kellay for their time, contributions and generosity during intermittent, and sometimes prolonged, periods of lockdown throughout 2020. Thank you Theatrum Mundi for the space to think and apply that thinking, and especially to Cecily Chua for her vision, and Lou Marcellin, Andrea Cetrulo and Elahe Karimnia for many additional conversations. Thank you to Marcos Villalba and Santiago Confalonieri for their foresight and design work. Thank you to Aleya James, Jane Haslam and Martha McGuinn for their generous thoughts late on in the edit. Thank you to Sriwhana Spong for the proofreading. And, thank you to John Bingham-Hall for his counsel and Marta Michalowska for making sense of all the material generated as part of the project.

Editorial: Marta Michalowska, Lou Marcellin
Design: Marcos Villalba, Santiago Confalonieri
Proofreading: Sriwhana Spong
Typeface: Neue Haas Unica
Printing: Colour Options

Ilustrations, including front cover: © Cecily Chua, 2021

Copyright © Theatrum Mundi, Susannah Haslam,
and individual contributors and rights holders, 2021

The right of Susannah Haslam to be identified as the author of this work has been asserted in accordance with Section 77 of the Copyright, Design and Patents Act 1988.

This work is subject to copyright. All rights reserved. No part of this publication may be reproduced, translated, stored in a retrieval system, or transmitted in any form or by any means, electronic or mechanical, without prior written permission from Theatrum Mundi.

Every effort has been made to trace copyright holders and obtain their permission for the uses of copyright material. The publisher apologises for any errors and omissions and would be grateful to be notified of any corrections that should be incorporated in the future editions of this book.

Theatrum Mundi
c/o Groupwork
15a Clerkenwell Close
EC1R 0AA
London, UK

Theatrum Mundi Europe
59 Rue du Département
75018
Paris, France

www.theatrum-mundi.org

This publication is part of Theatrum Mundi Editions, a quarterly series reflecting current streams and new directions in our research, led by our team and collaborators, and shared with our members. Editions are generously supported by the Friends of Theatrum Mundi.

Friends of Theatrum Mundi (please visit
https://theatrum-mundi.org/membership/)

ISBN : 978-1-9161864-7-7